D1710615

The Study and Teaching of History

Henry Steele Commager

Raymond H. Muessig
The Ohio State University

Charles E. Merrill Publishing Company
A Bell & Howell Company
Columbus Toronto London Sydney

The Study and Teaching of Social Science Series
Raymond H. Muessig, Editor

Published by Charles E. Merrill Publishing Co.
A Bell & Howell Company
Columbus, Ohio 43216

This book was set in Souvenir
Cover Design Coordination: Will Chenoweth
Production Coordination: Linda Hillis Bayma

Credits: Specific acknowledgments of permissions to use materials appear on page iv, which is to be considered an extension of this copyright page. Standard credit and source information appears in the *Notes.*

Photos: Cover by Gene Gilliom; Ray Muessig, 90, 92 (top left), 93 (top left), 102; The Ohio Historical Society, 92, 93, 106, 108, 110.

Library of Congress Catalog Card Number: 79-90846

International Standard Book Number: 0–675–08317–6

1 2 3 4 5 6 7 8 9 10—85 84 83 82 81 80

Printed in the United Sates of America

To
ALLAN NEVINS
with
Gratitude,
Admiration,
and
Affection

Acknowledgments

From THE FUTURE AS HISTORY by Robert L. Heilbroner. Copyright 1961 by Harper & Row, Publishers, Inc. Reprinted by permission of Harper & Row, Publishers, Inc.

From LEADING CONSTITUTIONAL DECISIONS, 15th ed. by Robert F. Cushman, Copyright 1977 by Prentice-Hall. Reprinted by permission of Prentice-Hall.

From AMERICAN CONSTITUTIONAL LAW: INTRODUCTORY ESSAYS AND SELECTED CASES, 6th ed. by Alpheus T. Mason and William M. Beaney. Copyright 1978 by Prentice-Hall. Reprinted by permission of Prentice-Hall.

From "The Homesick Buick" by John D. MacDonald. Copyright © 1950 by John D. MacDonald, reprinted by permission of Littauer and Wilkinson.

From "Everyman His Own Historian" by Carl L. Becker, in *American Historical Review.* Copyright © 1932 by the American Historical Association. Reprinted by permission of the American Historical Association.

From UNDERSTANDING HISTORY: A PRIMER OF HISTORICAL METHOD, 2d ed. by Louis Gottschalk. Copyright 1964 by Alfred A. Knopf, Inc. Reprinted by permission of Alfred A. Knopf, Inc.

Entry on page 6 from THE DICTIONARY OF MISINFORMATION by Tom Burnam (Thomas Y. Crowell). Copyright © 1975 by Tom Burnam. Reprinted by permission of Harper & Row, Publishers, Inc.

Reprinted by permission of the publishers, From Thomas A. Bailey, PROBING AMERICA'S PAST: A CRITICAL EXAMINATION OF MAJOR MYTHS AND MISCONCEPTIONS, VOLUME II (Lexington, Mass.: D.C. Heath and Company, 1973).

From THE DAUGHTER OF TIME by Josephine Tey. Copyright 1951 by Elizabeth MacKintosh, renewed 1979 R.S. Latham.

From MEMOIRS: SIXTY YEARS ON THE FIRING LINE by Arthur Krock. Copyright 1968 by Harper & Row, Publishers, Inc. Reprinted by permission of Harper & Row, Publishers, Inc.

Foreword

The Study and Teaching of Social Science Series is composed of six books, *The Study and Teaching of Anthropology, The Study and Teaching of Economics, The Study and Teaching of Geography, The Study and Teaching of History, The Study and Teaching of Political Science,* and *The Study and Teaching of Sociology.* In the larger part of every one of the six volumes, the social scientist was asked to deal with the nature and development of his field, goals of and purposes served by the discipline, tools and procedures employed by scholars, significant and helpful literature in the field, and fundamental questions asked and ideas generated by the academic area. Writers were challenged not only to provide solid subject matter but also to treat content in a clear, concise, interesting, useful manner.

Each of the six works in the series concludes with a chapter entitled "Suggested Methods for Teachers," which was written after reading and considering the complete manuscript by the individual social scientist.

In a number of ways, The Study and Teaching of Social Science Series resembles The Social Science Seminar Series (published in 1965) from which it is descended. The idea for The Social Science Seminar Series came to me in 1963, when the structure-of-the-disciplines approach in social studies education was receiving considerable attention in publications, meetings, and projects. At that time, social studies educators and supervisors and others were searching for substantive material concerned with the essence of academic disciplines and for down-to-earth ideas for specific classroom learning activities. They sought materials which would spell out and facilitate ways of translating abstract social science concepts and generalizations into concrete inquiry strategies that would be meaningful and appealing to children and youth. In the early sixties, some historians, economists, sociologists, anthropologists, political scientists, and geographers were trying to think of ways that others could teach respectable social science to elementary and secondary students about whom the academicians had little knowledge and with whom university scholars had no experience. And certain classroom teachers and others in professional education were informed with respect to human growth and development, child and adolescent psychology, theories of instruction in general and of social studies education in particular, day-to-day classroom organization and management, etcetera, and could work and relate well with younger pupils. These practitioners, however, readily admitted their lack of the kind of breadth and depth in all of the various social sciences necessary to do even an adequate job of defining and interpreting the disciplines. They frequently added that they had insufficient financial resources, time, energy, background in methods and media, creativity, and writing talent to produce for themselves and others the pages of requisite, appropriate, fresh, variegated, pedagogical alternatives needed to reach heterogeneous collections of learners at all instructional levels.

Thus, it seemed to me that a very real need could be met by a series of solid, practical, readable books where the content on each discipline would be written by a specialist in that social science and where the material on teaching strategies would be developed by a specialist in social studies education.

Now, some brief comments are appropriate regarding the revised and many completely new approaches for the last chapters in *The Study and Teaching of Social Science Series.*

The 1965 *Social Science Seminar Series* was designed primarily to assit K–12 teachers in the application of a structure-of-the-disciplines social studies theory in their classrooms. Since the needs and pursuits of the many users of the series have changed and become more diverse than they were in 1965, and since I, too, have changed in the ensuing years, this 1980 rendering is considerably more eclectic than its progenitor. Rarely is there a one-to-one relationship between a specific teaching method and a particular, overall theory of social studies education. Additionally, a myriad of instructional media may be matched with different philosophies and techniques. And, a single theory of social studies education need not be followed by an entire school district, by a whole school, by all of the teachers at the same grade level, or even by a given teacher throughout a school year with each of the students. The suggested methods in the last chapters of *The Study and Teaching of Social Science Series*, then, can be used as presented, modified to suit various classroom situations, adapted to complement different social studies theories, and altered to fit numerous goals and objectives. In the final analysis, a key test of a teaching method is the extent to which it touches the life of an individual learner in a meaningful way.

A Special Acknowledgment

When Charles E. Merrill Publishing Company expressed an interest in my plan to develop a series of texts in social science and invited me to submit a detailed proposal, I immediately asked Dr. Vincent R. Rogers (then at the University of Minnesota and now at the University of Connecticut) if he would join me as co-editor of the series and co-author of the chapters on instructional approaches. I worked with Professor Rogers on the refined plan that was sent to and approved by Merrill. Vin Rogers and I had written together previously in an easy, relaxed, compatible, mutually advantageous manner. We were both former classroom teachers who had become university professors of social studies education. We shared a feeling for the needs, interests, problems, and aspirations of students and teachers, had a serious commitment to the social sciences, and were familiar with a variety of instructional media. But, more than any other person I could find and attract as a co-worker on the endeavor, Rogers could translate significant ideas into functional, sequential, additive, meaningful, imaginative, enjoyable methods. Vin did his share throughout the entire undertaking, and he was responsible for the securing of all but one of the initial social science authors of the first version of this program. Our writing together on *The Social Science Seminar Series* went swimmingly, and we emerged even better friends than before.

When Merrill requested that Dr. Rogers and I revise and create new material for our concluding chapters for the six books in *The Study and Teaching of Social Science Series,* I anticipated the pleasure of a collaboration again. However, Professor Rogers already had too many previous commitments to undertake something as time consuming and demanding as this effort, and he had to withdraw, unfortunately. True to his generous personal and professional nature, Professor Rogers told me to use any or all of the ideas he and I had developed separately and together about fifteen years ago for these six volumes. We blended so well in the sixties, and so many things have happened since that time, that I doubt whether I could easily distinguish between our original suggestions anyway. Thus, my sincere thanks to Vin for his contribution to the first series and to this second undertaking.

Raymond H. Muessig

Preface

History, it seems, is more self-conscious than other disciplines, the historian more introspective than his colleagues in other areas of study and research. For a century now, historians have been asking themselves, publicly and eloquently, what is the nature of history? what is the use of history? what is it we are about? until the matter has become something of a public scandal. Chemists, biologists, and economists, engineers, economists, and jurisprudents are rarely assailed by comparable doubts; and if they are they tend to keep them to themselves.

Preoccupation with historical philosophy, historical criticism, historiography, is a relatively modern phenomenon, though there are of course antecedents stretching back to Plutarch or to St. Augustine. But it was not really until history became an academic subject—about a century ago—that such preoccupation became something of an obsession. Eighteenth century historians rarely questioned what it was they were engaged in. Giambattista Victo did, to be sure, but then he was generally ignored, but not Bolingbroke or Hume, Robertson or Gibbon, not Montesquieu or Voltaire, Muller or Raynal. They knew what history was—it was what they were writing. They knew what history was for, too; it was philosophy teaching by examples. Contrast with this self-confidence that long array of inaugural addresses by the Regius Professors of History at Oxford or Cambridge Universities, or the even more formidable series of annual addresses by the presidents of the American Historical Association, most of them confessing how troubled historians are about their profession.

The problem is not confined to that of identity or character; it has to do with function and method as well. Can history be impartial, can it be objective? Can it divorce itself from the tyranny of the present, of the nation, of the culture? Is the historian a judge—can he in fact avoid that function?—or is he a mere recorder, writing down "what actually happened"? It is possible *ever* to know "what actually happened," possible to establish a historical "fact" as one establishes a fact in chemistry or biology? Is there such a thing as historical causation, and can the historian ever know the causes of things?

These questions are, in all likelihood, unanswerable and these problems insoluble, and I have not, here, attempted to answer the questions or to solve the problems. I have tried, rather, to do two things: first, to throw some light on the questions themselves, to show what use they have, if any, for the study of history; and, second, to help students and teachers to get on with the job of study and teaching and writing. To suggest that we cannot profitably study or write history until we have answered all of our questions about the nature and the function of history flies in the face of common sense. It is as if we should say that we cannot paint pictures until we know the meaning of art and of beauty, that we cannot build universities until we know with certainty what is education, or that we should hold up the machinery of law and the courts until we have answered ultimate questions about the nature of law and of justice. Experience and philosophy both admonish us that not only the pleasures and rewards but even the understanding of any great subject come pretty much out of study and practice.

Because we cannot answer ultimate questions, it does not follow that we cannot answer immediate questions. I have tried here to formulate some answers to more elementary questions about the nature and the uses of history. I have suggested that we approach history as one of a number of ways of looking at life and experience, just as philosophy, literature, art, politics, are ways of reflecting on life and experience. None of these answers ultimate questions—though philosophy sometimes tries to—and for that matter none guarantees to answer even immediate questions. Rightly studied, however, they illuminate our understanding and broaden our sympathies.

This book is not, then, yet another contribution to historical philosophy, nor a handbook on historical methodology, nor an essay on historiography. Nor have I attempted to review the various "philosophies" of history; the study of the philosophy of history seems to me to belong rather in the province of the philosopher than that of the historian, and I subscribe to G. M. Trevelyan's observation that philosophy is not something you take to history, it is, or should be, something you carry away from history.

Henry Steele Commager

Contents

one

The Nature of History

The first thing to be said about *history* is that the word itself is ambiguous. It means two quite distinct things. It means the past and all that happened in the past. It means, too, the record of the past—all that individuals have said and written of the past, or, in the succinct words of Jacob Burckhardt, "what one age finds worthy of note in another." Sometimes it is said that these two things are in fact much the same: that the past exists only in our record of it, or our awareness of it, and that without such a record, there would be no meaningful past at all. Thus the great Italian philosopher-historian, Benedetto Croce, asserted that all history was contemporary history. There is, as we shall see, a germ of truth here. But this view is not so much wrong as confused and, in a sense, perverse. The past is not dependent on us for its existence, but exists in its own right. It happened even though historians failed to record it, just as the tree fell in the forest even though no one was there to hear the sound of its fall. History does not suddenly spring to life when some historian gets around to discovering it or recording it. The historian who clears up some puzzle about the past, or who discovers new material and fills in some gap in our knowledge of the past, does not in fact create the past, though he or she may recreate it. What happened, happened independently of the historian, and the consequences of whatever happened ensued independently of him or her. James Madison's *Notes on the Federal Convention,* for example, was not published until 1836; only then were historians able to penetrate into the very chamber of the Convention, to know, and to explain, what had occurred. Yet what had happened at the Convention—what delegates had said, for

1

example—had in fact happened and had made history. The consequences of the debates in the Convention did not wait upon the publication of Madison's *Notes*.

But if the debates in the Federal Convention were history, so was Madison's *Notes*. Just as what happened at the Convention had consequences, so the publication of the *Notes* fifty years later had consequences. It clothed with flesh and blood the skeleton of formal resolutions and conclusions with which historians had previously solaced themselves, and inaugurated both a more realistic and a more nationalistic interpretation of the Constitution.

What this suggests is that the historian, by discovering some lost ingredients in the past, or by illuminating dark areas of the past, can in a real way re-make the past. History is *there*—there in the fact that it did occur; there, too, in the conscious or the unconscious memories of individuals. The memory can be jogged, the consciousness can be stimulated, the image of the past can be changed. When historians do these things they make history.

History, then, is the past. History is also the memory of the past. Needless to say it is with the second of these meanings that we are concerned.

Let us consider history as memory.

For a people to be without history, or to be ignorant of its history, is as for a person to be without memory—condemned forever to make the same discoveries that have been made in the past, invent the same techniques, wrestle with the same problems, commit the same errors; and condemned, too, to forfeit the rich pleasures of recollection. Indeed, just as it is difficult to imagine history without civilization, so it is difficult to imagine civilization without history. As Frederic Harrison has written:

> Suppose that all knowledge of the gradual steps of civilization, of the slow process of perfecting the arts of life and the natural sciences, were blotted out; suppose all memory of the efforts and struggles of earlier generations, and of the deeds of great men, were gone; all the landmarks of history; all that has distinguished each country, race, or city in past times from others; all notion of what man had done or could do; of his many failures, of his successes, of his hopes; suppose for a moment all the books, all the traditions, all the buildings of past ages were to vanish off the face of the earth, and with them the institutions of society, all political forms, all principles of politics, all systems of thought, all daily customs, all familiar arts; suppose the most deep-rooted and sacred of all our institutions gone; suppose that the family and home, property, and justice were strange ideas without meaning; that all the customs which surround each of us from birth to death were blotted out; suppose a race of men whose minds, by a paralytic stroke of fate, had suddenly been deadened to every recollection, to whom the whole world was new. Can we imagine a condition of such utter helplessness, confusion, and misery?[1]

Clearly the concept of history set forth here embraces rather more than most historians would claim: the total record of the past—literature, law, art, architecture, social institutions, religion, philosophy, all indeed that lives in and through the memory of humankind. We need not embrace this imperial definition of history in order to agree that humans without memory would be bewildered and bereft. But memory, as we all know, is fitful and phantasmagoric. History is organized memory, and the organization is all-important. As organized memory, history takes almost innumerable forms, serves almost innumerable purposes. Let us consider some of the forms which it assumes and some of the purposes which it serves.

First, and if not most important, then most elementary, history is a story. That was its original character, and that has continued to be its most distinctive character. If history forgets or neglects to tell a story, it will inevitably forfeit much of its appeal and much of its authority as well. With the *Iliad* and the *Odyssey*, storytelling and history are so inextricably commingled that we do not to this day know whether to classify them as literature or as history; they are of course both. "The Father of History," Herodotus, had a story to tell—the struggle between the Greeks and the Persians—and he told it with immense verve. So, too, his great successor Thucydides, who gave us the story of the Peloponnesian War. Livy and Tacitus, the greatest of the Roman historians, were both superb storytellers, as are most of the leading modern historians, Voltaire and Gibbon, Carlyle and Macaulay, Prescott and Motley and Parkman. For, as Lord Macaulay wrote, "the art of history is the art of narration, the art of interesting the affections and presenting pictures to the imagination ... by skillful selection and disposition without indulging in the license of invention."

Here we come to the second quality of history. History is a story, to be sure, but it is not a made-up story; history draws on and excites the imagination, but it is not a flight of the imagination. It is a story of what happened in the past, or what the historian is able to recover and reconstruct of what actually happened. In short, history is a *record*. It collects and organizes such facts as are available and relevant, provides some kind of framework for them, and lays down the guidelines for the presentation. It supplies order, harmony, direction, for what might otherwise be a chaotic assemblage of miscellaneous facts.

There are, to be sure, serious limitations on the record, as well as on the ability of history to organize the record; we have to accept this without getting too disturbed about it. First, the record is, and is bound to be, fragmentary and complete. That is particularly true of the several thousand years of history before the invention of the printing press, and of the history of many of the peoples who even after the mid-fifteenth century knew not the art of Gutenberg—the American Indians, for example, or the peoples of Africa, whose history is largely unrecorded. For much of modern history the record appears to be more nearly complete—witness the miles of filing cabinets in the Pentagon and elsewhere, crammed with documents from the Second World War. Yet even here, needless to say, the record is incomplete. How can we know what happened, during the war years, to each of the more than twelve million Americans in uniform, to say nothing of the forty million or fifty million men and women of other countries who fought in the war? How can we know what happened to the hundreds of millions of civilians who were involved in the war, as participants, as victims, or as spectators? The record is incomplete for another reason: the limitations on the time, the energies, the intelligence, and the practical and technical resources of historians. No individual historian, not even the largest committee of historians, can read all those miles of documents, all the newspapers, all the personal records of the combatants of all the countries involved in the Second World War.

The record is not only irremediably incomplete, it is also lopsided and biased. How can it be otherwise? Much of it is wholly fortuitous. Our knowledge of the past depends pretty much on what happened to be preserved, and what happened to be preserved is only a minute part of the total record, minute and indiscriminate. Much of the record has perished by fire and sword—from the burning of the Alexandrian Library to the bombings of World War II; much of it has been destroyed by fanaticism, religious or national; much of it has simply been lost: thus of the forty volumes of Polybius' *Histories* only five survived, of the 142 books of Livy's *History of Rome* only thirty-five have survived! There is no logic here, no pattern; what has survived is largely a matter of luck.

Largely—but not wholly; for what has survived—or rather what has failed to survive—is also to some degree a matter of power. Justice Holmes used to say that Truth was the majority vote of that nation which could lick all others. History, too, is in part the verdict of the nation which licks others. Over the centuries history has been written by the victors, not the vanquished. It is the Romans who have written the history of the Punic wars, not the Carthagenians; the Christians who recorded the triumph of Christianity over paganism, not the pagans; the Spaniards who told the story of the conquests of Mexico and Peru, not the Aztecs and the Incas. One of the less amiable traits of victors, in the past, has been the deliberate destruction of enemy records and the silencing—often by death—of enemy historians.

The record which has come down to us, then, is not only fragmentary and selective; it is also biased. To be biased is as human as to err. Everyone knows that bias enters into even the simplest statement of events. No two stories of a family quarrel are ever alike; how should we expect that a score of accounts of the Battle of Gettysburg, or of the beginnings of the First World War, should be alike? History is, after all, not something which exists independently of humankind; it is something that comes to us filtered through the mind and the imagination of people.

Of all this, later, when we consider some of the problems of history.

History as a record consists of three states, or processes, usually so skillfully blended that they appear to be a single one. The first is the collection of what are thought to be relevant facts; but remember, what seems relevant to one person will appear irrelevant to another. The second is the organization of these facts into some coherent pattern; but remember, no two patterns are ever quite alike. The third is the interpretation of the facts and of the pattern; and certainly no two interpretations are ever quite alike. Now, all these processes flow into each other. The practiced historian is not ordinarily conscious of these separate steps any more than a skillful baseball player is conscious of the separate steps that go into a decision to strike at a ball. It is impossible to collect the facts in the first place without some theory of relationships among them; after all, what are you looking for? It is impossible to organize them into a pattern without some theory that dictates the pattern. And it is impossible to interpret them except on the basis of the material that has been selected and the pattern that has been drawn.

Neither collection nor organization is entirely under the control of the individual historian who is, in fact, wholly dependent on others for the material which he or she uses. No individual scholar can go very far in the collection of the material; mostly it has already been done, over the years and the centuries, by earlier scholars; by archivists who have preserved manuscripts and records; by devoted librarians who have assembled manuscripts and books, organized them, classified them, and protected them; by government officials who have provided for the preservation of court or legislative or diplomatic records; and by editors who have organized these. Imagine trying to write on the history of modern Parliament without Hansard's

Debates; imagine trying to write on the American constitutional system without the 375 or so volumes of the Supreme Court *Reports,* to say nothing of the thousands of volumes of lower court decisions; imagine trying to reconstruct the history of the French in Canada without the *Jesuit Relations;* imagine trying to interpret Thomas Jefferson without the help of—nay without total dependence on—the devoted editors who have collected his papers and made them available to other scholars.

It is interpretation—the third step in the organization of the record—which is most nearly individual and which therefore makes the highest demands upon the historian. Industry will go far toward solving the first problem, that of collecting the materials; common sense and judgment will contribute much to the second, the organization of the materials. But intelligence of a high order is required for the interpretation of the facts. The greatest of historians, certainly in modern times, have been the interpreters; and all the major modern historians have tried to be interpreters—that is, they tried to extract some meaning out of the inchoate raw materials of history, or to impose some philosophy upon it. Thus the great English historians: Clarendon and Gibbon and Hume, Macaulay and Froude and Lecky, Buckle and Freeman, Maitland and Lord Acton, and our own day Namier and Butterfield, and Father David Knowles and Veronica Wedgwood, and Denis Brogan and Winston Churchill. Thus in France, Montesquieu and Voltaire and Michelet and Taine and Tocqueville and Aulard; thus in Germany, Niebuhr and Ranke, and von Sybel and Treitschke and Lamprecht, and Burckhardt, and more recently, Meinecke and Rothfels. Thus in the United States Francis Parkman and John Lothrop Motley, Henry Adams and Vernon Parrington, Lawrence Gipson, S. E. Morison, and Allan Nevins.

Yet while interpretation depends on the accumulation of facts and their skillful organization, even the most prodigious industry and the most painstaking analysis do not guarantee a profound interpretation. That requires judgment, originality, imagination, and art. And this brings us to the third form, or character, of history— history as art. As Arthur Schlesinger, Jr., has said:

> All the elements of artistic form are as organic in historical as in any other kind of literary composition. There are limits on the historian's capacity for invention, but there need be none on his capacity for insight. Written history, after all, is the application of an aesthetic vision to a welter of facts; and both the weight and the vitality of an historical work depend on the quality of the vision.[2]

This is another way of saying that history is a branch of literature and that it serves some of the purposes and is governed by some of the principles of literature. Certainly most of the historical writing which we call great, and put into the category of the "classics," has literary distinction.

Literary history is not just a matter of fine writing. That can easily be overdone, and often is; the best style is plain and straightforward, as with Lincoln or Churchill in the realm of politics, or Trevelyan and Brogan among English historians, Douglas Freeman and Allan Nevins among American. Literary style is a matter rather of the tone, the color, the movement of the narrative; it is a matter of symmetry of structure, concentration of effort, architectural unity, and harmony, and the imagination which suffuses the whole. Listen to an example from a master of literary style who was also a master of historical fact, Francis Parkman, calling to our attention one of the paradoxes of Franco-American history:

> The French dominion is a memory of the past; and when we invoke its departed shades, they rise upon us from their graves in strange, romantic guise. Again their ghostly camp-fires seem to burn, and the fitful light is cast around on lord and vassal and black-robed priest, mingled with wild forms of savage warriors, knit in close fellowship on the same stern errand. A boundless vision grows upon us: an untamed continent; vast wastes of forest verdure; mountains silent in primeval sleep; river, lake, and glimmering pool; wilderness oceans mingling with the sky. Such was the domain which France conquered for civilization. Plumed helmets gleamed in the shades of its forests, priestly vestments in its dens and fastnesses of ancient barbarism. Men steeped in antique learning, pale with the close breath of the cloister, here spent the noon and evening of their lives, ruled savage hordes with a mild parental sway, and stood serene before the direst shapes of death. Men of courtly nurture, heirs to the polish of a far-reaching ancestry, here, with their dauntless hardihood put to shame the boldest sons of toil. [3]

While it is true that unless history is reasonably accurate and fair it should not be read, it is equally true that unless history is well written it will not be read. "The world at large," writes Allan Nevins, himself a distinguished practitioner of literary history,

> will sooner forgive lack of scientific solidity than lack of literary charm. The great preservative in history, as in all else, is style. A book of consummate literary art may abound in passages of bad history, but nevertheless carry generation after generation before it. It is useless to protest that Lord Clarendon was far too biased on the English Civil War; he will be read for centuries by all who savor a close-packed, pithy, eloquent style, full of graphic sketches of men and events. Motley is unscientific in his treatment of Spanish misrule in the Netherlands, but the world will continue to read Motley. If an historian were compelled to take his choice, fame might urge him to select the winged pen, rather than the Aristotelian mind, to choose Apollo against Minerva; but he may choose both. [4]

Justice Holmes used to say, finely, that "life is painting a picture, not doing a sum." So we may say that writing history is painting a picture, not taking a photograph. It is not enough to give photographic exactness; not even a photograph by Brady carries the impact of a painting by Goya, the "Massacre" for example. It is not enough to compile statistics; if it were, the *Statistical Abstract of the United States* would be, each year, our best historical volume. It is not enough to pile up mountains of historical and social details; if it were, the raw materials of newspapers would suffice for historical literature. It is not enough to put together strings of episodes and anecdotes, no matter how dramatic; picture magazines which do this dull rather than excite the mind. History must rest on statistics, embrace details, exploit drama, but it should control all of these ingredients as an artist controls the ingredients of materials and the elements of the subject—control them, master them, penetrate them with meaning and suffuse them with imagination.

Yet we must keep ever in mind that literary history, or history as literature, is not merely a matter of style—the winged word, the happy phrase, the brilliant epigram, the dramatist's art. The historian does not enroll, automatically, in the literary school when he or she writes well, nor suffer expulsion from that school when he or she writes in a flat or wooden style. Literary history is something more than a matter of style; it is something more than a matter of emphasis; it is a matter of philosophy.

The literary historian is primarily interested in recreating the past. He is, in a sense, a painter, and who can deny a Rembrandt, a Goya, a Longhi or Canaletto, a Reynolds, a George Catlin a place among historians? He is, in a sense, a dramatist, and who would deny Shakespeare or Molière or Holberg the title of historian? The literary historian employs his talents to conjure up what was once real and is now no more, and to excite the imagination of the beholder to see the past through his eyes. Like the painter, or the dramatist, he seeks to capture, for a moment, a brilliant, a famous, an endearing scene, to recreate a picturesque tableau, to paint a familiar portrait. He is Motley admitting us to the bedside of the dying Philip II of Spain; he is Prescott making us spectators of the bold attack across the causeway on Montezuma's great city; he is Michelet bringing us to our knees as we look on the tragic scene of the burning of the Maid of Orleans; he is Carlyle involving us in the heat of the battle of Rossbach.

All this is a far cry from the more prosaic and realistic purposes of the scientific historian. The gap between the literary and the scientific is not stylistic; it is deeper and more fundamental, a difference in the philosophy of history itself. The scientific historian is not really interested in recreating the past for its own sake, nor at pains to stir the imagination of the reader; indeed he is rather inclined to distrust the picturesque or the dramatic and even the individual. It is reason he wants to excite, not imagination, and as for the past he does not want to recreate it but to explain it. A great "technical" historian—Frederic Maitland, for example, who "turned the dust of archives into gold," or a Hastings Rashdall who made the medieval university as familiar as the contemporary, or Father Knowles, or S. E. Morison, can write with a style that sings and soars. But their primary purpose is not to stir the imagination but to solve problems. Was the "Mirror of Justices," upon which Lord Coke relied, authentic? How did St. Bernard triumph over the Cluniacs? Why did the students of medieval Bologna and Padua organize into Nations? Were the Puritans really hostile to music and the arts? Each of our historians has illuminated these problems with literary grace, but it was the problem that was important, not the grace.

Let us see how two distinguished historians, one "literary," the other "scientific," deal with the same situation. Here is Van Wyck Brooks, of all historians of American literature the most evocative, conjuring up for us the image of Nathaniel Hawthorne confronted by the spectacle of the New England Puritan in Rome:

> Was Hawthorne right in feeling that "it needs the native air" to give a writer's work reality? Rome had provided him with a fairy setting for the last of his own romances, — the last he was ever to finish, —the tale of Hilda, Miriam and Donatello, the dusky Miriam of the shrouded past and the delicate wood-anemone of the Western forest. This dance of Yankee girls and fauns and spectres was like a Pompeiian fresco or something immobilized on a Grecian urn. A bituminous light suffused it, as of an afternoon in the realm of shades. One caught in the shifting groups the magical, mythological grace of Poussin. One heard Mignon's song rising from the depths in the fitful measure of a wind-harp. Hawthorne had drawn enchantment from the Roman air; and yet, for all the spell of *The Marble Faun,* it was hardly comparable with *The Scarlet Letter* or *The House*

of the Seven Gables. The orchidaceous existence of most of the exiles seemed to bear him out in his distrust. One could dream forever in these Roman gardens, under the cypress and ilex, while all one's mental muscles atrophied. Norton, with his acute social conscience, his sense of a mission at home, probed under the surface of Italian life. The repressive political system disturbed him, and he had understood, from his own observation, the sorrows of Petrarch, Dante and Alfieri, who had mourned over their country and its degradation. Norton's critical faculties were alert; he had ridiculed the old romantic guide-books and the cold and pretentious work of the German painters who were dominant in modern Rome. He had cared for the realities of Italian life, as Greenough and Margaret Fuller had cared before him. The others did not wish to care. It was to escape from the prose of existence that they had left America. If their writing lost all grip and bottom, was not this the reason and the explanation?[5]

Here is what Francis Matthiessen has to say in his brilliantly written interpretation of the *American Renaissance:*

The danger of Brooks' impressionism is even more marked in the half paragraph which ... is the only space he has left for *The Marble Faun.* When he says that Rome had provided Hawthorne with "a fairy setting," and speaks of "the dusky Miriam of the shrouded past, the delicate wood-anemone of the Western forest," the flower that he envisages has nothing to do with Hawthorne's maturely bitter fruit....As a result of letting his attention be deflected from the work itself, he has made one of our few major artists seem less male and robust, much less concerned with important issues, than he was. Of all Hawthorne's heroines, Miriam leaves an impression least like the fragility Brooks describes....Her quick response to Kenyon's statue of Cleopatra (which is Hawthorne's response to Story's) is owing to her feeling within herself the operation of qualities equally fierce and turbulent....She is more deeply involved in a background of ambiguous guilt than any other of Hawthorne's characters; and his method of conveying this should be observed as a final aspect of his tragic technique, since it leads directly into the practice of James and Eliot.[6]

The differences here go to the very heart of the problem of the nature of history. Why does the literary historian want to salvage, to resurrect, to recreate, the past? It is because he is interested in the past for its own sake, interested in the drama, the spectacle, the pageant, interested in the actors and actresses. His is the view expounded by George Macaulay Trevelyan: "It is not man's evolution but his attainment that is the greatest lesson of the past and the highest theme of history."

The scientific historian is not interested in history for its own sake. He studies it because it is part of the evolutionary process, and it is that process which concerns him. He behaves, as Herbert Butterfield observes, "as though only those things are worthy of attention which gain importance from the fact that they led to something else." Like a good scientist, the technical historian wants to solve problems.

If the scientific historian has done much to illuminate the processes of history, it is the literary historian who has done most to expand its boundaries. For if we are to conjure up the past, not only its drama and its heroisms but its everyday simplicities, we cannot ignore the commonplace. To be sure, literary historians do yield to the seduction of the dramatic—witness a Prescott or a Motley, or, in our own time, a Guedalla or a Rowse. But Carlyle—who was himself irresistibly tempted by the dramatic—warned against this a century ago: "Mournful it is to behold what business called 'History' in these so enlightened and illuminated times, still continues to be. Can you gather from it ... any dimmest shadow of an answer to that great question: how men lived and had their being?, were it but economically, as what wages they got and what they brought with them?'' Carlyle did try to tell this, and so did his contemporary, John R. Green; somewhat later, so did the Dane Troels-Lund and the German Karl Lamprecht and the Frenchman Eli Halévy, and so did the American John Bach McMaster, who wrote clumsily enough. But we conclude as we began: ''literary'' history is not a matter of fine writing; it is a matter of the center of intellectual and historical gravity.

History is art; history is also philosophy. Lord Bolingbroke put it for all time when, drawing on the ancients, he defined history as ''philosophy teaching by examples.'' So almost all the great historians have thought, from Thucydides to Toynbee. History was philosophy in the Old Testament stories; it was philosophy in Thucydides, Polybius, Plutarch, Livy, and Tacitus among the ancients. Most modern historians accepted the Bolingbroke dictum as a matter of course: Montesquieu in his *Spirit of the Laws* and *The Grandeur and Decadence of Rome,* Voltaire in the *Age of Louis XIV,* Gibbon in *The Decline and Fall of the Roman Empire,* the Abbé Raynal in his many-volumed *History of the Indies,* designed, really, as an ''instrument of war'' against the Church and the Empire, and David Hume in his *History of England.* It is only recently that historians have attempted to discard this traditional function of history, and without much success. For philosophy, ousted from the front door, creeps back in through the side door. The public still wants philosophy with its history, and it is no accident that the most popular historians of our time—H. G. Wells and Winston Churchill and Arnold Toynbee, Georg Brandes and Oswald Spengler, Benedetto Croce and André Malraux, Salvadore de Madariaga and Raymond Aron, all wrote history as philosophy.

Yet few historians have been philosophers in any formal sense. They have relied on history, most of them, to teach simple moral lessons: the superiority of Christianity over other religions; the dangers of infidelity; the triumph of virtue over vice, or, in more sophisticated times, the futility of religious intolerance, the wickedness of kings, the depravity of man and the necessity of restraints upon his passions, the rise and fall of empires and the causes thereof—these and other lessons equally simple and equally dubious.

No one can seriously question the claim of history to be story, record, literature, and philosophy. What of its claim—or the claim of some of its more infatuated disciples—to be a science? History is invariably embraced in that loose term, *the social sciences,* but we do not know what that term really means. Are the social sciences in fact sciences at all, or is the word *science* used here rather in its original sense as *knowledge?*

It was the Victorians who first asserted that history was a science; that generation, so confident of its ability to create a science of humankind, embraced within this concept the science of society, economy, politics, law, and history. Thomas Buckle was sure that he had reduced history to a science by bringing it under the dominion of ''one glorious principle of universal and undeviating regularity'' —the law of Nature; while across the Channel Auguste Comte announced that ''history has now been for the first time systematically considered, and has been found, like other phenomena, subject to invariable laws.'' And at the turn of the century two Regius Professors at

Cambridge University, Lord Acton and J. B. Bury, intimated that if history were not yet a science it would inevitably become one. No modern Regius Professors now speak in such confident tones; yet the habit of thinking and speaking of history as a science is deeply engrained.

Clearly history is not a science in the sense that chemistry or biology are sciences. It cannot submit its data to scientific experiments; it cannot repeat its own experiments; it cannot control its materials. Wanting these, it will be said that of course history is not a science in any useful sense of the word. Yet it is equally clear that history uses or aspires to use the scientific method. That is, it tests all things which can be tested, and holds fast to what it finds to be true, insofar as it is able to make any findings at all. But how does history "test" things? What are the techniques of testing? How does it know when it has arrived at "truth" or even when it has achieved agreement of "facts"? The chemist does not inject his personality, beliefs, and prejudices into the chemicals which he uses in experiments; how does the historian rid his materials of such foreign ingredients? Indeed can the term *scientific method* ever mean the same thing in history that it means in the exact sciences? Should it perhaps give place to a more realistic term such as *critical method,* and should "scientific" history yield to "technical" history?

For there is this further, and sobering, consideration that the scientific method is valid—if at all—only in what might be called the formal and somewhat elementary realms of history, never in the really fundamental realms. Thus we can prove— scientifically if you will—that John Wilkes Booth did in fact shoot President Lincoln in Ford's Theater in Washington, on the night of the fourteenth of April, 1865. So far so good—but how far, and how good? For beyond that our science does not take us. Why did Booth do it? Who, or what, was responsible for his action? What were the consequences of the act? These, the really interesting questions, cannot be answered scientifically; they can hardly be answered at all.

Disillusioned with the claims of scientific history, some modern historians settled for what we may call *technical history*—a term coined by Professor Herbert Butterfield of Cambridge University. Let us not aspire too high; let us not try to formulate laws of history; let us not try to don the mantle of science! Let us rather take problems, one by one, as a biologist or a philologist takes problems one by one, the smaller the better, and works them out. If enough historians work tirelessly at enough problems, we may in time obtain a firm foundation upon which future historians can somehow rear the grand fabric of history.

The stigmata of technical history are by now sufficiently familiar. It distrusts the dramatic and prefers to catch history in a chemical solution, as it were, in a moment of arrested development, and to analyze it and dissect it. It eschews the narrative and turns instead to problems, though it does not really believe that any problems can be finally solved. It detests generalizations and is revolted by laws; it delights in the minute and the specific, and its characteristic form is the monograph. It has little interest in ideas and none at all in individuals, looking upon them as aberrations from some norm to be arrived at by the study of statistics, or distractions from the consideration of impersonal institutions. It is impatient with the notion of history as literature and rejects out of hand the idea of history as philosophy. And it has an irresistible fascination for the academic mind.

In all this, technical history has obvious association with modern developments in literature, art, criticism, and philosophy. In the second and third quarters of the twentieth century, literature too turned from its traditional concern with the narrative and the dramatic to the analytical and the descriptive, abandoned interest in plot and in characters and entangled itself instead with the impersonal, the subconscious, and the amorphous. "Let us record the atoms as they fall upon the mind in the order in which they fall," wrote Virginia Woolf. "Let us trace the pattern, however disconnected and incoherent in appearance, which each sight or incident scores upon the consciousness." Art, too, became increasingly abstract and impersonal, disdaining to tell a story and reluctant to present anything dramatic, heroic, or colorful: historical paintings and portraiture declined with historical narratives and biographies. Criticism addressed itself increasingly to the explanation of texts, while philosophy turned away from the great problems with which it had traditionally been preoccupied to problems of semantics. In the circumstances it was not surprising that the historian, bemused by the intricacies of technical history, should look with suspicion on history in the grand manner—history as narrative, as philosophy, as art—and settle for something that seemed to offer intellectual security.

Notes

1. Frederic Harrison, *The Meaning of History and Other Historical Pieces* (New York: The Macmillan Co., 1914), p. 5.
2. Arthur Schlesinger, Jr., "The Historian as Artist."
3. Francis Parkman, *Pioneers of France in the New World*, preface.
4. Allan Nevins, *The Gateway to History* (Garden City, N.Y.: Doubleday and Co., 1962), p. 379.
5. Van Wyck Brooks, *The Flowering of New England* (New York: E.P. Dutton and Co., 1936), p. 447.
6. Francis Matthiessen, *American Renaissance* (New York: Oxford University Press, 1941), p. 352.

two

The Varieties of History

There are as many kinds of history as there are historians, and each historian writes his or her own kind of history. And, as the historical philosopher Carl Becker observed, there are innumerable historians because every man is "his own historian." In one sense that is undoubtedly true, for everyone who tells a story recalling his childhood, or writes a letter describing a trip abroad or a baseball game or an exhibition is, after a fashion, a historian. He or she is doing, in a crude fashion, what professional historians do in a more sophisticated fashion: summoning up the past from whatever evidence is at hand, organizing the material, and dressing it up with drama and with art—even interpreting it all. And when the person puts himself in the center of the story he is giving us autobiography as well. Yet just as we do not describe everyone who writes a letter as a "writer," or everyone who draws a picture as an "artist, " so we should not describe everyone who records some past experience as a "historian." We do well to reserve the term for those who consciously undertake to reconstruct and present some segment of the past, and who do so with some semblance of craftsmanship, for more than private entertainment.

How is history to be told? No two histories are ever precisely alike, any more than any two poems or novels are precisely alike; if they were we should call it plagiarism. Yet over the centuries historians have worked out a number of patterns and these have come to be conventional, just as have patterns in poetry, music, or art. They are not fixed, or binding; there is room for variation and for experimentation (suggested, in our own day, by the film and television), and there is nothing either final or authoritative about the familiar patterns. But on the whole it is the traditional patterns, products of centuries of experience, that provided the best vehicles for history.

In a broad way these traditional patterns are the chronological, the geographical, the political, the cultural, the institutional, and the biographical. These are so familiar that they need little explanation or elaboration. The most elementary, and the most familiar, is the chronological, yet we speedily discover that even it presents problems. For where do you start? Start at the beginning, you may say, but that is not as easy as it sounds. There was a time, to be sure, when we could date the beginning with assurance: 4004 B.C., the date of the expulsion of Adam and Eve from the Garden of Eden. For centuries historians, as well as scientists, tried to fit their facts into this chronological straitjacket; not really until the eighteenth century did they find a way to extricate themselves from it. In the past century or so history has been able to move back a few hundred thousand years into something vaguely called prehistory, and properly to understand prehistory requires a knowledge of anthropology, paleontology, archeology, and many other things which few historians possess. Yet something is to be said for beginning if not at the outermost limits of prehistory, then with the Magdalenians who flourished in western Europe some ten to fifteen thousand years ago and who not only fashioned implements out of bone but left us the famous wall paintings in the caves of Lascaux in France and Altamira in Spain. If we prefer to leave this to the anthropologists, we are still confronted with the question of whether we start with "civilized" man in Mesopotamia about 3500 B.C., or in the Indus Valley, which boasted an advanced urban civilization some twenty-five hundred years before Christ, or perhaps with the Shang Dynasty of northern China, whose people had by that time already evolved a written language which was to endure until our own day.

The conventional thing is to begin with Egypt, Judea, Greece, and Rome. Here, after all, we can find the roots of our own civilization. And here, too, we can feel secure, for the territory has been surveyed, the guidelines and signposts all laid out. And how painless the transition to medieval history, traditionally dated from something called the fall of the Roman Empire and the transfer of the capital from Rome to Constantinople. Oddly enough, even with the recognition of that transfer Byzantine history was generally neglected; historically the center of gravity may have shifted eastwards, but most historians preferred to linger in the West, though they sometimes fell into the habit of calling these centuries of history the Dark Ages. With an almost audible sigh of relief, the historian struggled out of the medieval era into the twelfth century Renaissance, and then into that glorious Renaissance of the fourteenth to sixteenth centuries. This brilliant era was the threshold to modern history which could be dated from the discovery of the New World, or from Luther's famous Theses, as you wished. From then on the going was easy.

It was all far too simple, this division into ancient, medieval, and modern; indeed it was almost arbitrary. Its most obvious defect was its parochialism: these divisions did not really apply to history but to the history of the European West; they blandly ignored Asia, Africa, and the Americas, and assumed that nothing really counted except Europe, and that what was valid for Europe was valid for the rest of the globe.

There were other drawbacks. To apply names to long periods of history is to imprison them in our own concepts and expect them to live up to these names and concepts; we forget that the names themselves are arbitrary and parochial. People who lived in Periclean Athens did not think of themselves as living in "ancient" times, nor did the inhabitants of Tours or of London in the eighth century think of themselves as medieval people. To apply names, too, is to generalize; it is to suggest, if not to assume, that all who lived in the era of the Renaissance partook of what we now conclude to be the character of that era; that the Renaissance man was to be found alike in Florence, in Upsala, in the forest of Bohemia or the bogs of Ireland. Then there is the further difficulty that the designation and study of history by periods or eras tends to encourage the fallacious belief in sharp demarcation in history, and to blur the fact that eras of history blend and overlap just as the years blend and overlap in the lives of individuals.

Granted all this, there remains convenience. To study anything—literature or art, zoology or mathematics, we have to impose some kind of order upon it, divide it up and parcel it out. As long as we are aware of its limitations, the chronological order is as valid as any other and perhaps more convenient than any other. And may we not assert, too, that if we confine ourselves to a particular country—Britain or the United States—or to a coherent group of peoples and nations, there is much to be said for chronological distinctions? The Elizabethan Age, for all its connections with the past and the future, did have a character of its own, and so too did the Puritan era and the era of the Restoration. The Revolution did in fact divide the colonial era from the national, in American experience, and Czarist Russia differed sufficiently from Communist Russia that we are justified in distinguishing the two eras and studying them separately. We need not subscribe to the fallacies of the Zeitgeist philosophy to concede that youth and age have their distinct characteristics.

There is, of course, a very different chronological approach to history—to begin with the present, and work back. This method has its points, especially with the young. It is the way most youngsters find out about their family history: they begin with their parents and grandparents, and work back as far as information or rumor will take them. It is the way lawyers habitually work, from the present case to immediate and then to more remote precedents. Thus we can study such institutions as the political party, the presidency, the corporation, the labor union, the university, by tracing them back from their current character and conduct to their origins.

We tend, most of us, to look with misgivings on the writing of contemporary history, and therefore on this approach to history. The information is not yet available, we say, or it is impossible to achieve perspective so necessary to objectivity. True enough. Yet it is proper to remember that many of the greatest historians of the past wrote contemporary history. Thucydides lived through that Peloponnesian War whose history he relates; Tacitus wrote the history of his own times. Machiavelli's *History of Florence* is contemporary history, and Francesco Guicciardini's great *History of Italy* entirely so. Clarendon's *History of the Rebellion* is in part autobiographical; if Voltaire's *Age of Louis XIV* was not precisely contemporary history, Voltaire did live through twenty years of the Sun-King's reign. And who that reads the splendid pages of Winston Churchill's *World Crisis* or his *History of the Second World War* can doubt that in the hands of a master contemporary history can still be great history.

The geographical, like the chronological, organization of history has a kind of elementary simplicity about it that has long been irresistible to school teachers and writers of textbooks. The nineteenth century used to think of history as something that concerned only the European world, that is Europe, the Mediterranean, and the Americas. There was, to be sure, some fragmentary attention to the Near East at the time of Hammurabi and his code, or of the Moslem conquest of North Africa and of Spain, or during the era of the Crusades. From time to time the Orient would be smuggled in—now with the story of the Chinese discovery of gunpowder, now with Marco Polo, now with Clive in India or the opening of Japan by Matthew Perry, or the Boxer Rebellion—how illuminating that the uprising of Chinese against Europeans should be called a "rebellion." Africa, too, swam occasionally over the historical horizon—certainly when Europeans began to raid the hapless continent for slaves or to carve it up into colonies.

All of this represented a curious kind of historical astigmatism. Eighteenth-century historians—Voltaire, for example, and the Abbé Raynal—had seemed to break away from this European parochialism and "survey mankind from China to Peru," but even their gestures were artificial; clearly they were interested in the non-European parts of the globe only insofar as these may have impinged upon Europe. Only recently have historians generally abandoned the notion that history was something that happened to or affected the European world, and acknowledged that the non-European two-thirds of the globe is as important as the European one-third. Yet even this reappraisal of history is only partial and fitful. The history that is studied in the schools is still the history of Europe; the history that is read by the public is almost wholly European—a term which, of course, embraces both the Americas, and the British Commonwealth. This deeply engrained habit of looking at Asia and Africa—and sometimes even Spanish America—as mere appendages to Europe illuminates and explains many of the difficulties in international political and cultural relations today.

Here again, however, there is some logic in the tradition and the habit of the organization of history along geographical lines. It is not only convenient, it is helpful, to deal with the Mediterranean world as something of a unit, to deal with Europe as a unit, to deal with the Americas as units. The history of all peoples is interconnected, but geography and climate—the environment—determined the course of history quite as much as inheritance, and the historian may properly make environment his or her starting point, and accept it as his or her framework. There is danger here, to be sure: Henry Thomas Buckle (The History of Civilization in England) made geography not only the beginning but the whole of his interpretation of history, and failed spectacularly to make out a persuasive case. But if we use geography as an organizing device rather than as a philosophical explanation, we will find it useful.

A third method of organizing history, and one which derives in part from the geographical, is the political—a form of organization particularly endemic since the rise of nationalism. Thus we almost instinctively organize our materials into the history of Rome or of France, of the United States or of the Confederacy. Sometimes, for convenience, we combine groups of nations: the British Commonwealth, for example, or Latin America or Central Europe or Scandinavia. This political approach to history is, needless to say, almost wholly a product of modern history, for the nation-state is itself modern. Of all forms of historical writing the political is the most convenient and the most popular; almost all history is now studied in a political framework and that framework is even used, retroactively, to embrace the histories of peoples who flourished long before the rise of nationalism or the organization of the political state. The political approach to history is the most convenient because historical materials are customarily organized along national lines and by political and administrative departments—in the publications of government, of courts, in military and naval records, and so forth, and in the collection and organization of archive and library materials. It is convenient, too, because it makes relatively few demands upon the linguistic talents of scholars. It is popular because it appeals irresistibly to national pride, connects itself dramatically with the interest and the practical concern of readers, and with all that is most familiar, from stories in the nursery to studies in the schoolroom, from politics to patriotic festivals.

In the circumstances it is not surprising that most modern historians have accepted E. A. Freeman's dictum that "History is past politics, past politics present history." Whatever the inadequacies of the political view, it can be said that a habit of history—it is too much to call anything so nearly instinctive a philosophy—which has given us such literary monuments as Macaulay's *History of England*, Michelet's *History of France*, Johann Müller's *History of the Swiss Confederation*, Peter Münch's *History of the Norwegian People*, Henry Adams' brilliant *History of the United States During the Administration of Jefferson and Madison*, more than justifies itself. Whatever the limitations of national history, historians can, and do, overcome them and even turn them to advantage. Whether history written without nationalist preconceptions, or outside the nationalist framework, can improve on national history remains to be seen.

The student should keep in mind that the political approach to history is fraught with danger. It inculcates a narrow and parochial view of history, and tempts both historian and student to indulge in chauvinistic patriotism. It reads back into the past the artificial divisions of modern nationalism, and exaggerates the role of politics and diplomacy at the expense of other elements in history. By pouring everything into the political crucible, it melts down the rich ores of culture, religion, social and economic institutions into a single slab distinguished only by the political impress which is stamped upon it.

A fourth form, or pattern, of history is the cultural. It is not easy to define *cultural history*. It is the history of the mind and character of a people, of the major ideas which appeared to dominate a society or an age, of the institutions with which we associate the conduct and faith of men. Probably no other form of history makes greater demands upon the scholar; probably none is more fascinating when those demands are satisfied. The requirements of cultural history are not satisfied—as some misguided historians appear to suppose—by a naked record of what was written or painted or composed or built by a society during a particular era: during these years Mozart and Beethoven were composing sonatas, during these Kant and Kierkegaard thought deep thoughts, during these Renoir and Manet developed Impressionism—that sort of thing! No, the cultural historian is called upon to know, understand, and explain the ideas and interests of a whole generation, sometimes in many different societies, and to trace their manifestations in the whole fabric of history. As ideas are almost always cosmopolitan, he or she is required to cut across the barriers of nation and language and perhaps even of time as well. You can tell the story of the disputed election of 1876 in wholly isolated terms, but you cannot do justice to the Centennial Exposition of 1876 without bringing in romanticism, science, art, industry, and a dozen other subjects as well. The cultural historian is required to know the history of many countries, to be familiar with art, literature, philosophy, and science, and to be wise enough to fuse all these into a synthesis.

This is not easy, for where political history has, or appears to have, a certain simplicity and clarity of outline, cultural history is sprawling, distracted, and amorphous. What is it, after all? Is it anthropology, as in Frazer's famous *Golden Bough* or in Lewis Morgan's *Ancient Society?* Is it sociology, as in the fourteen volumes on *Daily Life in the North in the Sixteenth Century* by the Danish historian Troels-Lund, or in Charles Booth's *Life and Labour in London?* Is it economics, as in Rostovtzeff's *Economic History of Rome?* Is it religion, as in Mandell Creighton's *History of the Popes* or the multivolumed *History of the Papacy* by Ludwig von Pastor, or Anson Phelps Stokes' three volumes on *Church and State in the United States?* Is it art, as in Jacob Burckhardt's *Renaissance in Italy* or Berenson's *Painters of the Northern Italian Renaissance* or Rewald's volumes on the *Impressionists* and the *Post-Impressionists?* Is it education, as in Rashdall's *History of Medieval Universities* or Sandy's *History of Classical Scholarship?* Is it law, as in Holdsworth's fifteen volumes on the *History of English Law* or Charles Warren's *Supreme Court in United States History?* Is it science, as in Needham's *History of Science in China* or Lynn Thorndike's *History of Magic and Experimental Science?* Is it military, even, as in Fortescue's *History of the British Army* or Oman's *History of the Peninsular Campaign* or Douglas Freeman's *R. E. Lee* and *Lee's Lieutenants?* Certainly it is literature, and cultural history has traditionally adopted literature as its most convenient vehicle: the examples here are too numerous to rehearse.

Some historians have been bold enough to try to put all of these things together, to provide a synthesis which embraces the whole thought and character of a society. Thus, for example, John Addington Symonds' seven volumes on the history of the *Renaissance in Italy,* thus Alfred Zimmern's *Greek Commonwealth,* thus Paul Hazard's interpretation of *European Thought in the Eighteenth Century,* thus Werner Jaeger's study of Greek culture, *Paideia,* thus Vernon Parrington's controversial *Main Currents in American Thought,* which embraces almost every expression of thought except the philosophical.

All of these have in common an interest in ideas rather than in "events," and a resolution to cut across the barriers which divide politics, law, economics, society, philosophy, science, and art. These are admirable objectives, but they are difficult to realize. It is far easier to write a history of the Sherman Anti-Trust Act of 1890 than to trace the complex and elusive elements that explain German, English, and American Transcendentalism. But if the rigors and risks of intellectual history are great, so too are the rewards. It is gratifying to reflect that the writings of such cultural historians as Burkhardt, Symonds, Leslie Stephen, and Troels-Lund, now almost a century old, flourish with undiminished vigor and influence new generations.

The most interesting development in recent historical study has been the emergence of what we have come to call *cultural anthropology*—a study, or discipline—which has flourished especially in America. There are, to be sure, respectable antecedents: eighteenth century studies such as Voltaire's *History of the Morals and Customs of Nations* and Raynal's vast *History of the Indies* could both be classified as essays in cultural anthropology. So too could perhaps the greatest book ever written on America, Tocqueville's *Democracy in America* which, in a severely formal fashion, embraced most of the social and psychological characteristics now

explored by the cultural anthropologists. Other nineteenth century cultural historians, too, borrowed heavily from anthropology: examples are Lewis Henry Morgan's pioneering *Ancient Society* or Frazer's classic *Golden Bough* or Wilhelm
Grönbeck's neglected *Culture of the Teutons* or Thorstein Veblen's epoch-making
Theory of the Leisure Class. It is upon the work of such historians, and upon the
writings of sociologists like Herbert Spencer and Lester Ward, that the new school of
cultural anthropologists build. Perhaps their methods and techniques are more
original than their ideas. To the highly "civilized" societies of America or Britain they
apply the techniques originally developed for the study of "primitive" societies—the
societies of Samoa or the Trobriand Islands or the Pueblo Indians. With what they
hope is scientific objectivity they turn their anthropological and sociological spotlights
on the habits, customs, rites, and ceremonies of Middletown or Plainville, U.S.A., of
Manchester, or Copenhagen, or the Vaucluse. They have little interest in the familiar
subjects—politics or literature or philosophy or art—but address themselves rather
to such matters as toilet training, dating patterns, the play and games of children, the
sexual practices, eating habits, prestige concepts, and racial attitudes of adults.

Perhaps the chief value of all this to the historian was that it gave a new dimension
to that familiar and traditional enterprise, the study of national character. The
nineteenth century had been fascinated by this concept, and such books as Tocqueville's *Democracy in America* and Emerson's *English Traits* had given it respecta-
bility, while W. E. H. Lecky, the historian of eighteenth-century Britain, had gone so
far as to insist that national character was the only subject worthy of study. But as,
increasingly, in the twentieth century, nationalism and race lent themselves willingly
to the most evil purposes, historians became wary of generalization about national
character, and eventually all but abandoned the notion that there was any such
thing. After all, they said, humans are more alike than they are different, and national
traits are fortuitous rather than inherent; the whole idea of national character is
romantic and probably pernicious.

Now, however, with the rise of the cultural anthropologists, the stone which the
builders rejected became the cornerstone of the new history. As the historians
hastened to abandon the field of cultural nationalism, the cultural anthropologists
moved in. If there was no national character, there were national characteristics.
Soon national character—and particularly the American character—was subjected
to intensive statistical study by students of public opinion, child training, educational
practices, class and caste, sports and games, popular culture and popular prejudices,
language and idiom, and power struggles. And on the basis of their findings—so one
of their spokesmen asserted—"the statistical prediction can safely be made that a
hundred Americans will display certain defined characteristics more frequently than
will a hundred Englishmen comparably distributed as to age, sex, social class, and
vocation."

Cultural anthropology has a further contribution to make to history; it helps to
democratize history. No one can deny that history is, and always has been, dis-
criminatory and exclusive. It prefers to dwell with monarchs rather than with their
subjects, with popes rather than rural vicars, with generals rather than with privates,
with statesmen rather than civil servants, with captains of industry and titans of
finance rather than workingpeople and clerks. It delights in the spectacular, the
dramatic, and the sensational—battles, crises, famines, natural catastrophes, heroic

deeds, and foul crimes. The annals of the poor, we are assured, are short and simple; mostly they are nonexistent.

As long as history depends on the written record, and the record that survives, all this is natural and almost inevitable, for the vast majority of humankind have left no records. The historian who wishes to find out how the great mass of plain people lived is forced to rely on such artifacts as happen to survive—tools, instruments, clothing, folk art and folk ballads, or on such records as have been made by churchmen or by officials—births, marriages, deaths, records of military service, the findings of courts, the statistics of the tax collector, and so forth; in modern times these miscellaneous records are supplemented by the newspaper. In the hands of skillful and imaginative historians like Troels-Lund who recreated *Daily Life in the North in the Sixteenth Century,* or Ferdinand Gregorovius who traced the *History of the City of Rome in the Middle Ages,* such data come to life; but mostly historians have neglected them.

The cultural anthropologist is not, for the most part, interested in recreating the historical past, but the materials which he or she assembles and exploits do illuminate that past, for qualitatively, at least, his or her interests parallel those of the social historian. The cultural anthropologist is not concerned with the great and the powerful, the machinations of diplomats, the rhetoric of statesmen, the strategy of generals, except as these happen to illustrate popular traits. His or her interest is, by logical necessity, directed to the habits of play and courtship, of work and of worship, to family relationships, popular preferences in food and clothing, popular ideas of right and wrong. Because the commonplace generally has deep roots in the past, the data which the cultural anthropologist so carefully assembles from such miscellaneous sources becomes, sometimes retroactively, the data of history.

What is new about the cultural anthropology of our day that distinguishes it from the social and cultural history of the past two centuries? First, perhaps, that at last cultural anthropology is doing what historians and sociologists long promised to do, but rarely did: depicting the daily lives of ordinary people at every level of civilization.

Second, borrowing perhaps from Freudian psychiatry, the cultural anthropologists see in preliterate peoples the intellectual and moral ancestors of modern or civilized societies. They realize that what is overt and conscious in early society lingers on as covert and unconscious in the most sophisticated of peoples. As such, they decide that the study of early beliefs and superstitions illuminates and even explains the psychological life of individuals and societies today.

Third, modern students of cultural anthropology do not differentiate between what have in the past been called "primitive" and "civilized" societies, but accept each society as independent, unique, and possessed of a culture as self-sufficient as that of the highly sophisticated societies of the West. What this belief means is that the anthropologists neither condescend to the societies they study nor try to change them, but rather try to learn from them. Thus there is a sharp departure from the library-oriented research of the Troels-Lund or a Frazer. Ever since Malinowski— indeed for that matter since the American Lewis Morgan—anthropologists have gone out into the field and lived, sometimes for years, with their subjects, trying to enter into their minds and their ways of life.

Fourth—and perhaps most profitable, as it is certainly most interesting—the cultural anthropologist of our time brings to the study of the character of Western societies the same insights, tools, and techniques that have been employed for the study of earlier societies. It is here that cultural anthropology departs most dramatically from the cultural and intellectual history that existed all through the nineteenth and twentieth centuries. Modern cultural anthropologists are not as interested in formal "thought"; they more often follow ideas such as the way the Russians and the Japanese raise their babies; the differences in play patterns between American and Chinese children; the significance of the "inner-directed" and the "outer-directed" individual; the pressures that exaggerate individualism and competitiveness and those that discourage these traits; and dating patterns and sex patterns among the young (and among the old, too). Thus they most often study indices to national character.

Finally, in all this inquiry, segments of society heretofore neglected—children and women, the poor, the humble, the ignorant, even the delinquent—are accorded the place of honor, whereas the great, powerful, and learned are regarded as interesting chiefly in relation to the deference or disdain with which society regards them. It has been the cultural anthropologist who has placed the child and the family everywhere in the very center of the social stage. A notable literature has emerged in the past two decades, ranging from Erik Erikson's study, *Childhood and Society,* and Philippe Ariès's *Centuries of Childhood* to Robert Cole's incisive volumes on the impact of poverty on American children of our time, *Children of Crisis,* and to Jean Piaget's volumes, *Child and Reality* and the *Language and Thought of the Child.* And thanks in large part to the influence of Freud, and to the growing permissiveness of our society, subjects long excluded from polite literature, even scholarly literature, now command most conspicuous attention. Where Victorian educational literature, for all its preoccupation with the importance of physical culture and of the notion of *mens sana in corpore sano,* never mentioned sex or the reproductive system, much of the literature on childhood and adolescence today sometimes seems to mention nothing else. Sex provided the clue for Malinowski's studies of the people of the South Seas; it was a prominent part of G. Stanley Hall's four volumes, *Adolescence;* it was the chief theme of Margaret Mead's *Male and Female;* and sex is pervasive for the interpretation of the American character in Francis K. Hsu's *Americans and Chinese* (1970). And it can be argued that the most influential and possibly the most valuable contribution to cultural anthropology of our time are the reports of Alfred Kinsey and his associates in *Sexual Behavior in the Human Male* and *Sexual Behavior in the Human Female.*

Secularization, the laws of nature, the idea of progress, the influence of climate, the all-encompassing force of evolution, economic determinism—in the early years of the twentieth century, these great ideas that did so much to shape the character of history were joined to the insights of psychiatry, which we associate with one of the intellectual giants of our age, Sigmund Freud.

Psychology is very old, though not by that name. Psyche herself appears in Greek mythology as the beloved of Eros; her conquests and her empire have expanded enormously in modern times. The term *psychology* appeared first in 1749, in David Hartley's *Observations on Man;* it was another hundred years until the emergence of the term *psychiatry,* and then it was in connection with medicine; it will not be forgotten that both William James (whose great book on psychology in 1890 inaugurated the modern study of that subject) and Sigmund Freud were trained in medicine. Actually, what we now call *psychohistory,* in one form or another, is very old and familiar. Thucydides' account of the appeals by Nicias and Alcibiades to the passions of the Athenians in the debate over the Sicilian expedition is a little masterpiece of psychology. Plutarch's portraits of the Greeks and the Romans sought to penetrate to the psyches of these illustrious men; in his sketches of the Caesars — the sadism of Caligula, the hysteria of Claudius, the perverseness of Nero — Suetonius anticipated something of modern psychiatry. And since Machiavelli's subtle analysis of the nature of power, many modern historians — Gibbon, Carlyle, Karl Lamprecht, and Henry Adams among them — have indulged themselves and their readers in rich psychological speculations. In 1904 James Harvey Robinson of Columbia University asserted that "the progress of history must depend largely, in the future as in the past, upon the development of cognate sciences...perhaps above all psychology," and that same year Henry Adams wrote in *Mont-St.-Michel and Chartres* of the intellectual and artistic life of the High Middle Ages as a kind of sublimation of the love for the Virgin. But until Freud, none of these commanded the techniques of psychiatric research.

Freudian psychiatry grew out of Freud's experiences with his patients, and so was long confined to the individual. Therefore, its insights were, and remained, more useful in biography than in history, and today it is most evident in such studies as Erik Erickson's *Young Man Luther* and *Gandhi,* Leon Edel's *Henry James,* David Donald's *Charles Sumner,* Halvdan Koht's *Life of Ibsen,* Hajalmar Helweg's psychiatric study of that tortured soul, *Hans Christian Andersen,* or Fawn Brodie's *Jefferson,* or Bruce Mazlish's *In Search of Nixon.* Freud came to believe that the life of the race recapitulated the psychological life of the individual, and that what was conscious in primitive man persisted as unconscious in civilized man. As the sexual drive was the most universal and powerful of all forces operating on human beings, their development could be understood in terms of the efforts of organized society to control, direct, express — and repress — that drive. It was to explore the implications of these theories that Freud wrote many of his later works: *Totem and Taboo* (1913), *Civilization and Its Discontents* (1929), and the highly controversial but enormously influential *Moses and Monotheism* (1939).

If much that was unconscious but powerful in civilized man was conscious and overt in the ritual and magic of primitive societies, then those who wanted to understand what appeared irrational or inexplicable in modern man could turn with profit to the study of primitive peoples. The great James Frazer of the multivolumed *Golden Bough* had already seen something of this, and so had psychologist-anthropologists like Bronislaw Malinowski, with his pioneering studies of the sexual life of the Trobriand Islanders, or E. A. Westermarck, whose *History of Human Marriage* was almost the first scholarly work of anthropology and psychology to bear on the sexual life of both primitive and civilized peoples. Soon a new school of cultural anthropologists, including Franz Boas, Ruth Benedict, Margaret Mead, and Alfred Kroeber were concentrating on the study of the American Indian or the natives of the South Sea islands, with new insights borrowed from the realms of psychiatry of contemporary peoples. Clearly those now classic studies by Alfred Kinsey, *Sexual Behavior in the Human Male* and *Sexual Behavior in the Human Female,* owe an immense debt to the new school of cultural anthropologists.

If Freud's impact on conventional history has been meager, his influence on the study of culture has been prodigious. It has contributed greatly to our understanding of irrationalism, mass hysteria, paranoia, the prejudices about class, sex, and race. Most of these contributions have come from psychologists and sociologists, to be sure: thus Erich Fromm's penetrating study, *Escape From Freedom,* which cast so much light on the psychology of totalitarianism; thus Bruce Mazlish's *Hitler;* thus Hannah Arendt's classic essays, *The Origins of Totalitarianism* and *On Violence;* thus Jay Lifton's sobering study of the impact of disaster on a community, *Death in Life: Survivors of Hiroshima;* thus David Riesman's *Lonely Crowd,* with its perspicacious analysis of the shift in the American character from inner- to outer-directed man. Contributions of historians have tended to focus increasingly on the more ostentatiously irrational chapters of American history—Salem witchcraft, for example; or fanaticism, North and South, that paved the way to open conflict in 1861; or the hysteria of the 1940s that made possible the Japanese concentration camps; or the phenomenon of mass paranoia that partially explains the success of Senator Joseph McCarthy in the fifties. Yet how does one ultimately explain the state of mind and emotions that sustained the institution of black slavery, the theory of white supremacy, and the persistence of the myth of the unique purity of southern womanhood (which has figured so prominently in southern fantasies for a century and a half), all of which linger in, and contribute so much to, the irrationality in the current discussion on the issue of school busing? Thomas Jefferson, who saw everything, observed that "the whole commerce between master and slave is a perpetual exercise of the most boisterous of passions," and sexual fantasies about the relations between black and white disturbed the thinking of southern apologists and of northern abolitionists in the decades before the Civil War. Certainly Wilbur J. Cash's *Mind of the South,* Winthrop Jordan's *White Over Black,* Stanley Elkins' *Slavery,* and Eugene Genovese's profound and compassionate *Roll, Jordan Roll* have drawn heavily upon the findings of psychiatry. Psychiatry has illuminated, too, such miscellaneous chapters of American history as the role of the cowboy as a symbol of virility, the persistence of anti-intellectualism, the nature of the search for identity vis-a-vis the mother country in the first half of the nineteenth century, and the persistence of the paranoid style in American politics—a subject to which the gifted Richard Hofstadter contributed so richly.

Psychohistory has not yet, however, vindicated its claims to have added a distinctly new dimension to historical (as distinct from biographical) understanding. It provides insights, but those insights are perceptive rather than conclusive. A gifted psychiatrist like Erik Erikson can probe deeply into the motivations of a Luther or a Gandhi, but it is not so easy to probe the motivations of a hundred thousand or a million people, especially when (as is commonly the case) the data are fragmentary and elusive and can never be submitted to scientific test. The historian stands on firm ground when he or she is aware of the forces of irrationality and assigns to them a role in history, but the historian is on treacherous ground when trying to explain the origins or the motivation or the impact of irrationality. Nor is it entirely clear that fascination with motivation is advantageous rather than distracting to the student of history. Even our own motives for the simplest of actions—let us say the choice of a college, a career, a spouse—are almost infinitely complex; how difficult it is to be sure of the motives of Henry VIII, Napoleon, Leonardo, Rockefeller, or Hitler. Again, whether Henry VIII was motivated by lust, caprice, religious conviction, or reasons of state, and whether John D. Rockefeller's benefactions were inspired by ambition, vanity, or the desire to distract public attention from his predatory activities makes really but little difference: what does make a difference is what happened.

It is difficult to know whether quantification should be considered as a new idea or only a new technique, or even whether it is new. In one sense it is very old indeed. Historians have always counted—the years of a dynasty, the number of soldiers in an army, the drachmas or livres or pounds in the treasury—and they have always recognized, too, the importance of counting.

Quantification is new neither in practice nor in philosophy. What is new is, first, that the historian now has available prodigious quantities of statistical data drawn from census, social security, welfare, military, medical, commercial, and financial records; and second, thanks to new mechanisms like the computer, this data can be used and mastered with efficiency, accuracy, and rapidity. Taken together, these developments constitute a change analogous to (though not equal to) the changes introduced by the invention of printing in the fifteenth century, the emergence of scientific library classification in the nineteenth, and electronic devices like the tape recorder in the twentieth. These data amount to a quantitative advance so remarkable that it achieves qualitative significance. For historians now have at their command a body of empirical data vastly greater and incomparably more readily available than at any time in the past, and along with this they have mechanisms to assure a rigor, an accuracy, and a concreteness heretofore unknown in historical writing. "To have any validity at all," Lawrence Stone has said, "conclusions about social movements must have a statistical basis." Conclusions now coming out of the famous Sixieme Section of the French historical institute, which addresses itself so energetically to problems of demography and statistics, and from similar groups in England and the United States have an authority acknowledged by scholars everywhere.

Yet for all its revolutionary techniques, quantification was, philosophically, a return to the ideal that inspired Leopold von Ranke and his followers to believe that they could reconstruct the past "as it actually happened." Indeed, what had been merely a romantic hope became instead a scientific possibility. For—so the quantitative historians believed—with the aid of the computer, the IBM card, the tape recorder, and other technical devices, it was possible to reconstruct some segments of the past brick by brick, as it were, and stone by stone. Now historians could substitute facts—hard facts, authenticated facts, well-mannered and well-disciplined facts— for the mixture of speculation, inference, and conjecture that had passed for history among uncritical historians of earlier times. Now, for the shadowy and subjective past of the classical and romantic schools, the quantifiers were prepared to substitute a past born of the marriage between the data bank and the computer and guaranteed to be objective. It was, once again, that "noble dream" against which Charles A. Beard had fulminated, but it was a dream that the technicians proposed to realize.

And it was true that in some areas, most of them real and public, the quantifiers could discover almost everything they needed of a quantitative nature. Quantification could recover statistics of births and deaths, disease and longevity, marriage and family, from a thousand parish records; it could give an accurate table of voting, county by county and precinct by precinct, in all modern elections; it could trace the vicissitudes of farm production and farm prices, mortgages and foreclosures, and correlate these with voting or migration; it could record the increase in literacy, and the great number of functional illiterates who remain; it could determine how many hours children spent in front of a television screen, and what the public thought it thought about the impact of television on its children. It could explore both horizontal and vertical mobility in discrete populations, or the relationship of revolutions and counterrevolutions to religious affiliations, or the correlations of union membership with voting patterns, or levels of education with sexual habits and prejudices. What could it not do? What it did not even pretend to do was to explain the statistics that it so hopefully submitted. But then, that was the business of the philosopher.

Even as the new school of quantifiers was intoxicated with its triumphs, doubts and misgivings emerged. Quantification was all very well, but its usefulness, so it was asserted, was limited, and it might even prove "counterproductive." Though it is as yet too soon either to vindicate or to refute the criticism, we must take note of it.

First, it is asserted that the quantitative approach to historical problems is lacking both in subtlety and in sophistication and in the all-important comparative dimension, and that while it no doubt provides an impressive body of accurate facts, it often points to misleading conclusions. Consider, for example, the flood of monographs on voting in the American colonies and states in the eighteenth century. Some of these reveal that most adult white males (and in New England there were few who were not white) were entitled to vote in New England town meetings, and substantial numbers in colonial or state elections; others suggest that only 15 or 20 percent of these males could or did in fact vote. Now if you take your stance in the present, when all men and women over eighteen are (in law at least) permitted to vote (though notoriously they do not), that looks like a pretty limited democracy. But if you take your stance in the eighteenth century and do not confine yourself to the American scene, you note at once (what you do not need quantifications to reveal) that on the European continent no one voted at all—except in the Swiss cantons— for there were no elections, and that even in Britain less than 200,000 persons were entitled to vote and far fewer, in fact, did. Thus, left to themselves, your computerized figures might lead the unwary to the conclusion that eighteenth-century America was a very limited democracy, whereas in fact it was incomparably the most democratic society in the world. To be sure, the quantifiers would point out here that it is the business of historians to educate the "unwary"; to make clear that laws are not always rigorously enforced, or that considerations other than those of legal qualifications affect voting, or that an examination of voting in New England towns or Virginia counties is not supposed to be an exercise in comparative Western history. Alas, the responsibility of explaining these things often goes by default.

Second, it is alleged that while quantification may provide the data for judgment, it is no substitute for judgment, and that those who use it are almost irresistibly tempted to believe that if there are only enough facts, the facts will speak for themselves. Thus quantification puts a premium on the continuous accumulation of data. In this it ignores the law of diminishing returns. Certainly mircofilms of ten midwestern newspapers of the Populist era are a great deal more valuable than microfilms of only two or three, but it does not follow that microfilms of one hundred are ten times as valuable as microfilms of ten. The accumulation of data can in fact be self-defeating; there is, in any event, no very impressive correlation between quantitative accumulation and qualitative interpretation. Thus, to take two very different examples, Tocqueville's interpretation of equality in Jacksonian America, arrived at entirely by the deductive method, is still more valuable than most of the more scientific studies of class structure produced with the aid of quantification; Troels-Lund's enchanting fourteen volumes on *Daily Life in the North,* written in the last quarter of the nineteenth century, wholly without benefit of any of the new techniques, remains almost a century later incomparably the best study of its kind in any historical literature.

To be sure, in the hands of skillful quantifiers—the members, for instance, of the famous Sixième Section in Paris, who have so successfully explored problems of demography in medieval France, the fluctuations in the production of grain, and the causes of the Vendé counterrevolution of the 1790s—the use of statistics is both critical and judicious, and the results illuminate areas of history heretofore in shadow. So, too, with Alfred Kinsey's use of the techniques of the interview and of statistical analyses in his now classic volumes on human sexual behavior—reports that have had a profound and lasting influence on the public attitude toward sexual habits and on legislation. But the Kinsey reports, which appeared in 1948 and 1953, were without benefit of computers, and nothing of equal importance has emerged in the last two decades.

Third, quantification tempts the historian, almost irresistibly, to concentrate on the modern or even the contemporary scene, for it is in the modern period that surely an abundance of records can be found. There are, of course, data for quantification in the town records of colonial New England (see John Demos' study of the Plymouth colony) or in the parish records of seventeenth-century England (see Peter Laslett's *The World We Have Lost*); it is possible to draw important conclusions from a study of votes in the state and national legislatures in the Federalist era (see David Fischer, *The Revolution of American Conservatism*), and as far back as 1939, Lawrence Harper's intensive analysis of customhouse records in the American colonies added new understanding to the workings of the *The English Navigation Laws.* But the archival and statistical riches of the modern era act as a magnet to younger historians who are in a hurry and who, in any event, are more interested in the modern than the medieval scene, while the relative scarcity of statistical data on, let us say, Carolingian demography or Icelandic civilization or literacy in the Germanies in the eighteenth century discourages investigation into those areas.

Yet modern science and technology can chalk up triumphs even in the most ancient fields. Willard Libby's stunning discovery in 1947 that he could date organic matter with considerable exactitude as far back as forty thousand years by measuring with a Geiger counter the amount of radiocarbon that remained in it was the greatest contribution to archaeology since those two remarkable Danes, C. J. Thomsen and J. J. A. Worsaae, first hit on the three-level system of prehistoric civilizations—the Stone Age, the Bronze Age, and the Iron Age—in the early years of the nineteenth century. And, more recently, the IBM 705 managed to index, in a few weeks, some 30,000 words extracted from the Dead Sea Scrolls, a task that might otherwise have dragged on for a generation.

A fourth reservation about quantification has to do with style rather than sub-stance. It associates itself eagerly with psychohistory, sociological history, and linguistics, and adopts a language, or a jargon, that is always difficult and sometimes incomprehensible.

Finally, the most serious—and perhaps the most obvious—criticism of quantification is that it acts as a kind of self-fulfilling prophecy; it almost irresistibly channels historical research into those areas and toward those problems that promise to lead themselves to the quantitative approach. Thus in the realm of politics it produced not the *Federalist Papers* but studies of voting patterns; thus in the realm of class relationships it produced not *Democracy in America* but Lee Benson's admirable but little-read *Concept of Jacksonian Democracy;* thus in the realm of law it gave us not Holmes's *Common Law*—still a classic one hundred years later—but C. H. Pritchett's studies of the Roosevelt Court and the Vinson Court; thus in the realm of slavery, Robert Fogel and Stanley Engerman's *Time on the Cross.* As Arthur Schlesinger has observed, the quantitative approach .

> claims a false precision by the simple strategy of confining itself to the historical problems and materials with which quantitative techniques can deal, and ignoring all the others as trivial. The mystique of empirical social research, in short, leads its acolytes to accept as significant only the questions to which the quantitative magic can provide answers. As a humanist I am bound to reply that almost all important questions are important precisely because they are *not* susceptible to quantitative answers.

What is clear is that the tools and techniques of quantification have added almost immeasurably to the tools of historical research; they are no substitute for the "conceiving imagination."

There is another form of history, one that parallels and contributes to all the others: history as biography. A large part of history has come down to us in the form of biography. Many of the most familiar stories of the Old Testament are biographical—the story of Joseph and his brethren, for example, or of David and Naboth's Vineyard, or of Job. Plutarch was doubtless the greatest practitioner of history as biography, and his *Parallel Lives of the Greeks and the Romans,* as we know, deeply influenced the Founding Fathers. It was Thomas Carlyle who put the biographical theory of history most strongly:

> Universal history, the history of what man has accomplished in this world, is at bottom the History of the Great Men who have worked here. They were the leaders of men, these great ones, the modellers, patterns, and in a wide sense creators of whatsoever the general mass of men contrived to do or to attain.... In all epochs of the world's history we shall find the Great Man to have been the indispensable savior of his epoch;—the lightning, without which the fuel would never have burnt.[1]

Though few modern historians have been willing to accept this extreme interpretation of the role of great men in history, many have written as if they would like to. English and American literature are peculiarly rich in biographies: Boswell's life of Dr. Johnson, for example, or Lockhart's multivolumed tribute to Sir Walter Scott, or James Anthony Froude's four volumes on Carlyle, or John Morley's solid monument to Gladstone and his slighter but more brilliant studies of Voltaire and Rousseau, or Winston Churchill's six volumes on his ancestor, the Duke of Marlborough, or George Macaulay Trevelyan's glowing story of Garibaldi, while in American literature such books as Beveridge's *John Marshall,* Douglas Freeman's *R. E. Lee,* Arthur Link's *Wilson,* Leon Edel's *Henry James* come to mind. Now, all these biographies have one thing in common: they are history as well as biography. They place their subject against a rich and elaborate historical background, relate him to the great historical ideas and events of his time, use him to illuminate the history of an age. They all belong to what we may call the Life and Times School, which contrasts sharply with the personal and psychological school which we associate with such writers as Lytton Strachey or André Maurois or the American, Gamaliel Bradford.

History never gets very far away from biography; even such austere subjects as law or science are illuminated by biographical approach. Nothing, to be sure, quite comes up to Holdsworth's massive fifteen-volume *History of English Law,* but it is impossible to understand even the history of English law without knowing the men who made it and pronounced it: Lord Coke, Blackstone, Mansfield, Bentham, Brougham, Eldon, for example. It is even more futile to try to understand the history of American constitutional law without taking into account the personalities of John Marshall and Joseph Story, Justice Field and Justice Holmes, and it is no accident that American literature is particularly rich in judicial biographies. And while specialists can approach the history of science through the technical literature on that particular science, for the layperson it is the biographical approach that is most rewarding. While the history of American science remains to be written, Americans are fortunate in a handful of first-rate biographies: Lynde Wheeler's *Willard Gibbs,* A. Hunter Dupree's *Asa Gray,* Brooke Hindle's *David Rittenhouse,* Wallace Stegner's biography of Major Powell, *West of the One Hundredth Meridian,* and Edwin Martin's *Thomas Jefferson, Scientist.*

For reasons easy to sympathize with, biography has always been the most popular form of history. It is pleasant to read, dramatic, and colorful; it personalizes and simplifies complex problems; it illustrates the promise of Longfellow's *Psalm of Life,* that

> Lives of great men all remind us,
> We can make our lives sublime,
> And, departing, leave behind us,
> Footprints on the sands of time.

It is for precisely these reasons that so many professional historians—particularly those who practice "technical" history—look upon biography with a deep suspicion. Nothing, said the great Lord Acton, "causes more error and unfairness in man's view of history, than the interest which is inspired by individual characters." And Lewis Namier, perhaps the most influential of modern British historians, insisted that the study of biography was a kind of historical kindergarten; the historian should not distract himself with the study of individuals, but address himself rather to those great forces of politics and the economy which determined the course of history or those great institutions where the influence of the individual was negligible.

Still another form of historical analysis is enunciated by Robert F. Berkhofer in his book *A Behavioral Approach to Historical Analysis.* Berkhofer supports the borrowing of social science theories, concepts, and techniques for historians to better understand the complexities of the past. Berkhofer suggests that behavioralism provides the best answers to historical questions for it includes knowledge from several of the social sciences: psychology, sociology, and anthropology. This approach is more complex than that of quantification but, when combined with it, can provide the foundation for a more sophisticated concept of humankind's present or past activity.

The behavioral approach, like quantification, contributed to the "new" history based largely upon the techniques of the social sciences. Such approaches could assist in the discovery of the "grass roots" of history. Historians could now study the lives of the inarticulate and minorities who left no great abundance of literary works or written records. As a result of these social science techniques, state and local history or studies in microcosm took on new intellectual importance. Stephan Thernstrom's *Poverty and Progress: Social Mobility in a Nineteenth Century City* tested the conception of nineteenth-century America as a land of opportunity, and Paul Kleppner's *The Cross of Culture: A Social Analysis of Midwestern Politics, 1850–1900* drew the focus away from national studies so common to the period before the 1960s. Kleppner discovered quantitatively that religion, ethnic group, and personal value systems consistently affected local-level voting behavior more than "great national issues" like the tariff. The publication of local history took place with the idea of illuminating large problems in American history. A further expansion of this microanalytic trend is the recent interest and emphasis on family history. Family history is an even smaller fragment of the group or class emphasis so identified with state and local history. The works of John Demos, Phillip Greven, Jr., and Kenneth Lockridge best exemplify this type of history, which seek to use the family as a determinant of behavior. Encouragement for this approach to history came with the overwhelming success of Alex Haley's *Roots,* which spurred new research in genealogy and gave new credibility to that particular aspect of history.

Tackle any major problem in history and you will discover at once that you cannot understand it in isolation, but that you are involved in politics, international relations, science, technology, economics, psychology, and morals. If you want to understand James Fenimore Cooper's America you will find yourself inescapably involved in the history of romanticism, Indian ethnology, and the controversy over democracy, land laws and land policies, and a score of other matters. To understand the Supreme Court decisions in *Munn* versus *Illinois* requires some familiarity with the history of agriculture and of railroads in America, the politics of Supreme Court appointments, and the history of English as well as of American law. The fact is that men and women do not live in compartments labelled "politics" or "law" or "religion" or "economics"; they live in all of these simultaneously. The same people who write constitutions and draft laws also build houses, marry and raise families, work at machines, write books, go to church, and fight wars.

There is no danger of parochialism or of narrowness in history; properly studied each chapter of history opens out onto ever-new chapters. Nor can good history be neatly labelled and pigeon-holed. Is Parrington's *Main Currents in American Thought* history or literary criticism? Who cares? Where do you classify Leslie Stephen's *English Thought in the Eighteenth Century?* It is intellectual history; it is philosophy and theology as well. Turn to Morley's biographies of Voltaire and Diderot and Rousseau, and you are plunged into the very vortex of the most exciting intellectual controversies of modern times. If you wish to know Thomas Jefferson you are required to immerse yourself in all his interests: in politics and law, philosophy and religion, literature, art, and architecture, agriculture and gardening, history and natural history, anthropology and ethnology, education and libraries, and a dozen other things as well. History is as all-embracing as life itself and the mind of humankind.

Notes

1. Thomas Carlyle, *On Heroes and Hero-Worship,* 1841, Lecture I.

three

The Study of History

Reading History

Does it make any difference what history we read? Justice Holmes once said that any subject is great when greatly pursued. A dull scholar can make even *Hamlet* or the Declaration of Independence dull, while a luminous mind like John Livingston Lowes can write a fascinating work, *The Road to Xanadu,* on the sources of Coleridge's poem, and a powerful mind like Walton Hamilton can write an original work on a single phrase of the Constitution—"commerce among the several states"—which throws new light on *The Power to Govern.* Admitting this, it still does make a difference what the scholar writes or the student reads. While, no doubt, all historical subjects are equal, some are more equal than others, and while all eras of history are interesting, as it turns out, the Renaissance, Elizabethan England, the French Revolution have a richness, a variety, a complexity which have excited students for generations, and that excitement has communicated itself in great literature.

This is, after all, the common sense of the matter. Doubtless every child is beautiful in the eyes of its parents, and we have on the authority of a hundred poets that every mistress is lovely in the eyes of her lover. The rest of the world, however, does not necessarily accept these verdicts, but abides by its own standards of beauty or virtue or interest. Certainly a biography of our old friends John Doe and Richard Roe is not as interesting as a biography of Abraham Lincoln or Robert E. Lee, and all the art in the world could not make it as interesting. No matter what genius a historian lavishes on a history of the Tariff of 1884, he or she cannot really make that subject as exciting as the history of the writing of the federal Constitution, nor is the history of Harrod's store, splendid as that London emporium doubtless is, quite in a class with the history of the Spanish Armada. It is no accident that almost all business biographies— purchased at no matter what cost—are failures, or that almost any book on Jefferson or Disraeli or Winston Churchill is interesting.

From this it follows that the argument for studying Periclean Athens or Renaissance Florence or the federal Constitution or the American Civil War is a circular one: for generations affluent minds have lavished their attention upon these and similar subjects, and the student can be sure, therefore, of a rich storehouse on which to draw. Just as we tend to study those areas of art which produced great artists—a Leonardo, a Raphael, a Michelangelo, for example—or those chapters of the history of music which recount the careers of a Bach, a Hayden, a Mozart, a Beethoven, so we may be forgiven if we prefer to study those chapters of history which have produced or inspired the greatest historians.

For purposes of study, then, there are some preferred chapters of history. Study those chapters of history which, for one reason or another, have attracted first-rate minds and talents to their exposition. Study the history of ancient Greece because some of the greatest poets and dramatists and historians of all time recorded that history, and because for over two thousand years Greece has exercised an irresistible fascination over the minds of men. Study the Italian Renaissance because that study will take you to Florence, Siena, Rome, Milan, Venice, and because countless rich minds have been there before you and celebrated what they found: Cellini and Machiavelli and Castiglioni and Guicciardini, for example, among the contemporaries, and Jacob Burckhardt and John Addington Symonds and Ferdinand Schevill and Bernard Berenson among the moderns. Study the history of Puritanism or the making of the federal Constitution or the Jeffersonian era because you will assure yourself of association with men of superior talents and characters, and because you will be guided, in turn, by historians who combine literary and scholarly talents of a high order. That cannot be said, for example, of the study of the Hayes or the Harrison or the Coolidge administrations.

A second rule for the study of history is equally elementary: read for pleasure and for intellectual excitement. History opens up new worlds, just as geological exploration and science open up new worlds. Needless to say history embraces both of these, so that through the pages of history we can share the excitement of discovery. The many volumes of the Hakluyt Society, in their enchanting light blue bindings, enable us to sail with Francis Drake and Martin Frobisher and Captain Cook to far quarters of the globe; through the pages of Beazley's great *Dawn of Modern Geography* we can share the excitement of the unfolding of the globe, the beginnings of cartography, the discovery of the compass and astrolabe; with the greatest of all geographer-historians, Alexander von Humboldt, we can enter into a new *Kosmos*. Nowhere is the story of geographical discovery more exciting than in America; with Bernard De Voto we can follow *The Course of Empire* from New- foundland to the Pacific; or we can concentrate on single chapters of that story by familiarizing ourselves with the exploits of the eccentric John Ledyard of Connecticut, or immersing ourselves in the *Journals* of the Lewis and Clark expedition. The history of science, still in its infancy, is no less exciting, Joseph Needham's volumes on *Science and Civilization in China*—Herbert Butterfield has called it the most important historical work of our generation—opens up new worlds to even the most sophisticated; and so does George Sarton's five-volume *Introduction to the History of Science*. If these seem too formidable there are fascinating interpretative studies such as Giedion's *Mechanization Takes Command* or Loren Eiseley's recreation of *Darwin's Century* or Daniel Boorstin's *Lost World of Thomas Jefferson* or Lewis Mumford's critical *Technics and Civilization*.

History has depth as well as scope. It enables us to enter into the minds and characters of the great figures of the past with a degree of intimacy unimaginable for our own day or our own society. In this it is like compounding family history a thousand-fold; it permits us to know the pasts of other societies, even those which have been swept away by time such as the Etruscan, the Aztec, the Inca, the Viking. It plunges us into the most enthralling eras of human experience and enables us to know some of their greatest characters—a Leonardo, a Jefferson, a Goethe, a Lincoln—more intimately even than their friends and companions knew them. Through history we can follow them in their every deed and, through their letters, their journals and diaries—records rarely available in their own day—we can follow them almost in their every thought. This is one of the most gratifying of all rewards of history; perhaps only in great imaginative literature do we get anything comparable.

It is important then, in studying history, that we choose great companions. We would not willingly fritter away our lives on dull people, and there is no reason why we should fritter away our intellectual energies on the dull and the trivial. Concentration on the trivial makes for pedantry or for superficiality. Concentrate, then, on what historians have found to be significant. To be sure, historians are not infallible; to be sure, an original mind can often find drama and significance in what has long been neglected or deemed of no consequence. After you have become familiar with some of the great epochs of history, and some of the leading historians, it is time to do a bit of exploring on your own.

A third rule for reading history is to read systematically. Nothing is more time-consuming and, in the end, more surely calculated to consume interest as well, than to read miscellaneously and indiscriminately; that is like reading whatever magazine the airline flight attendant happens to give us. In history, as in most matters, order, system, and discipline are essential. No one who flits from the piano to the violin to the flute without mastering any one of them will become a musician; no one who dabbles in French, German, Italian, and Spanish without mastering one of them will become a linguist. The literature of history is almost infinitely voluminous: there are at least twenty thousand volumes dealing with the French Revolution and in all likelihood quite as many bearing on the American Civil War, and it requires the Folger Library of a quarter-million volumes to do justice to Shakespeare and his times. To "dip into" every era of history, or the history of every country, is to court lunacy.

What is wanted is system and seriousness. First, then, read solid works, not books made up of fluff and stuff. The butterfly technique—sipping at whatever is attractive—is the kind of self-indulgence which speedily leads to satiety. If you are interested in the American Civil War start with Douglas Freeman's four volumes on *R. E. Lee* and then go on to his three volumes on *Lee's Lieutenants*. By the time you have studied these, you should have a deep and ardent feeling for the war, and you should have too an awareness of having lived with a great man—and to have seen him through the eyes of another great man, Douglas Freeman. Then you can go on to other solid works—Allan Nevins' monumental *Ordeal of the Union,* for example, which carries you from the Compromise of 1850 to Appomattox in eight rich volumes, or Bruce Catton's dramatic recreation of life in the Union Army in his three volumes on the Army of the Potomac, or Sandburg's lyrical tribute to Lincoln—there are six volumes altogether. By then you will be able to appreciate Stephen Benet's epic poem, *John Brown's Body,* still in some ways the best evocation of the war. Historical novels, too, have a contribution to make, and there is no other chapter in our history that has attracted so many good novelists or inspired so many readable novels. You can immerse yourself in novels like De-Forest's *Miss Ravenel's Conversion,* in Winston Churchill's *The Crisis,* or in more modern and more realistic recreations of the war like Evelyn Scott's *The Wave,* McKinlay Kantor's *Andersonville,* or Michael Sharra's *Killer Angels.*

By this time you will perhaps have had your fill of secondary works and will want to turn to the sources themselves—the vast library of letters and diaries and memoirs bequeathed by participants, the lively accounts of journalists and travellers, not to mention the reports of the many artists—the immense mass of official papers and records, political, diplomatic, and military, far too voluminous for any one historian to master. To find your way through this labyrinth of source material would be a desperate task but for the happy fact that others have been there before you, have surveyed it and mapped it and marked out the paths.

You are not set adrift on a limitless sea of diplomacy: Owsley is there to guide you with his *King Cotton Diplomacy* and E. D. Adams with his two-volume study of *Great Britain and the American Civil War,* and a score of other scholars as well. You are not left to wander aimlessly through the records of the battle of Gettysburg; a dozen biographers, a score of military historians, are ready to provide guidance. You are not left to conjure up for yourself the causes for the defeat of the Confederacy; a hundred scholars have speculated on just that question, a hundred books provide not only the theories and explanations but notes and references which direct you to the source material and enable you to arrive at your own conclusions.

Or suppose it is Thomas Jefferson who has caught your fancy—there is no one more rewarding, no one who better fulfills the promises he holds out on first acquaintance. The literature here, too, is immense, and you will do well to begin with one of the many good biographies—that by the French-American scholar, Gilbert Chinard, for example, or the three fascinating volumes by Marie Kimball, or the still incomplete biography by Dumas Malone. Once you know what most interests you in Jefferson you will want to turn to his own astonishingly voluminous writings. There are two older editions of the writings, and one magnificent edition still under way—some seventeen volumes published—edited by the greatest of Jefferson scholars, Julian Boyd. Now you will be ready for some of the almost innumerable monographs dealing with particular aspects of the life of this versatile genius. There is, for example, Karl Lehmann's wide-ranging essay on *Thomas Jefferson, American Humanist,* or Fawn Brodie's *Jefferson,* or James Bryant Conant's lectures on *Jefferson and the Development of American Education,* or Edwin Martin's study of *Thomas Jefferson, Scientist,* or Fiske Kimball's book on *Thomas Jefferson, Architect,* or Edward Dumbauld's *Thomas Jefferson, American Tourist.* If you want politics, there are the volumes which the incomparable Henry Adams devoted to Jefferson in his

History or the two volumes by the diplomat-historian Claude Bowers, *Jefferson and Hamilton* and *Jefferson in Power,* or C. M. Wiltse's *Jeffersonian Tradition in American Politics.* Charles A. Beard has investigated the *Economic Origins of Jeffersonian Democracy;* Leonard White has done a definitive job on the administrative side of the Jeffersonian years, *The Jeffersonians;* and Merril Petersen has traced the *Jeffersonian Image in the American Mind.*

But this is, in a sense, only the beginning. You cannot understand Jefferson in a vacuum; you must know his associates and disciples; you must know his intellectual companions and his philosophical antecedents; happily these are well worth knowing. James Madison was, for almost fifty years, Jefferson's disciple and friend—the friendship has been explored by Adrienne Koch in a book on the two men. You will want to read Irving Brant's six-volume biography of Madison and to read some of Madison's own essays and letters in the older edition by Gaillard Hunt or in the new edition of the *Papers* now under way. Albert Gallatin, too—the Swiss *philosophe* who cast in his lot with America and became, in time, Jefferson's Secretary of the Treasury—was a member of the Jeffersonian circle: you can read his life in a masterly biography by Henry Adams, and his *Writings* are edited, in three volumes, also by Adams. You can scarcely think of Jefferson without his lifelong friend—and sometime antagonist—John Adams: they worked together for fifty years and died, dramatically, on the same day, precisely fifty years after the Declaration of Independence. To know Adams is almost as big a task, and almost as interesting, as knowing Jefferson. There are good biographies by Gilbert Chinard and Page Smith; there is an admirable study of Adams' political thought by Edward Handler, and Zoltan Haraszti has set forth his relation to the French *philosophes* in *John Adams and the Prophets of Progress.* You will of course want to read Adams himself: the *Diary* and *Autobiography* have already been republished, in four volumes, and the correspondence and miscellaneous writings will soon be available in the new edition of the Adams papers edited by Lyman Butterfield. But to know Jefferson you must know not only his associates, but his intellectual and philosophical antecedents. Turn then to the five-volume catalogue of his library which Millicent Sowerby has edited; to the elaborate annotations in Boyd's edition of the *Papers;* to the many monographs on Jefferson's French associates by Gilbert Chinard; and to studies of the Enlightenment by John Morley, Carl Becker, Ernst Cassirer, Paul Hazard, Basil Willey, and a score of other interpreters. By now you will realize that to do justice to Jefferson is the work not of a year but of a lifetime, but that is true of almost *every* really great or spacious subject.

A fourth rule in the study of history is always to work from the particular to the general, never from the general to the particular. General works—outlines of this or that, surveys of everything—are almost guaranteed to rot the brain. The method of history is the method of science—inductive and empirical; it is the method of law—the case study; it is the method even of art—to start with the study of anatomy, with the mastery of paints, or of stone. Begin, then, with the particular—with an individual or an episode or an institution—and work from there to more general subjects. Are you interested in the United States Constitution? Start with the document itself, read the debates in the Federal Convention (they have been admirably edited by Max Farrand) and the debates in the ratifying conventions as well, the so-called *Elliot's Debates.* Read and re-read *The Federalist* papers, incomparably the most profound commentary on political philosophy and on constitutionalism written in this country: there are several good modern editions. Now you are ready to go on to constitutional history. A good book of documents will give you many of the essential laws, proclamations, presidential addresses, and judicial opinions. A good history of the Supreme Court—that by Charles Warren, though by now out of date, is unquestionably the best—and a few biographies such as Beveridge's voluminous *Marshall* or Charles Fairman's *Justice Miller* or Alpheus Mason's *Chief Justice Stone* or Max Lerner's edition of the *Mind and Faith of Justice Holmes* will go a long way toward clarifying the intricacies and complexities of the constitutional system. Genuine scholarship would of course require that you immerse yourself in the decisions of the Supreme Court—the very stuff and substance of our constitutional law and history; there are some 375 volumes of these, and here you will clearly need expert guidance. Fortunately, a score of casebooks which bring together the leading decisions are at hand. By the time you have studied the Constitution and the Court intensively you will have familiarized yourself not only with the American constitutional system, but with most of the issues of American politics, economy, and society.

The average reader, it is fair to say, gets his or her sense of the past not through the writings of formal historians, but through the pages of fiction directly or, in recent times, translated into films and television dramas. This is natural enough; the story comes before history in the life of the race, as in the lives of individuals. Biblical stories came before Josephus' *History of the Jews,* and the *Iliad* and the *Odyssey* before either Herodotus or Thucydides, and it is not only children who have learned the history of England from the stories of King Arthur and his knights of the Round Table, or from Froissart or Chaucer, but their parents as well. Winston Churchill (who himself wrote a historical novel) said that he learned all of his English history from the plays of Shakespeare, and Francis Parkman's debt to Cooper's *Leatherstocking Tales* is notorious, while G. M. Trevelyan has paid handsome tribute to the influence of Walter Scott on his own historical writing. "Fiction is truth's elder sister," wrote Rudyard Kipling, with pardonable exaggeration. No one in the world knew what truth was until someone had told a story. So it is the oldest of the arts, the mother of history, biography, philosophy, and, of course, "politics."

Cooper and Scott, and Kipling, too, remind us that the historical novel is very much a nineteenth century invention. It began—there were of course antecedents—with Walter Scott and John Galt in Scotland, with Fenimore Cooper and William Gilmore Simms in America, with B. S. Ingermann in Denmark and Victor Hugo in France and Alessandro Manzoni in Italy. These were, for a generation and more, the most widely read of modern writers, providing the whole civilized world with stereotypes of historical characters and episodes. The historical novel spread from England throughout Europe and became a standard expression of historical nationalism. Almost every major writer tried his hand at it: Thackeray and Bulwer-Lytton and George Eliot and Disraeli and even Dickens in England; Victor Hugo and Stendhal and Dumas and Flaubert in France; Gustav Freytag in Germany; Sienkiewicz in Poland; Manzoni in Italy; Pushkin, Turgenev, and Tolstoy in Russia; and in Spain Perez Galdos whose *Episodios Nacionales* filled no fewer than forty-six volumes.

Nowhere did the historical novel flourish more vigorously than in the United States. Almost all the major writers turned to history for their material: Irving, who was both a historian and a novelist, and his friend James Kirke Paulding, Cooper and

Hawthorne and the almost forgotten De Forest and the prolific E. Marion Crawford, and the southerners Beverley Tucker and John Pendleton Kennedy and William Gilmore Simms; even the historians Motley and Parkman managed to squeeze in one historical novel apiece. Harriet Beecher Stowe gave us *The Minister's Wooing* and many other historical panels, and Howells did not fail to conjure up frontier Ohio, and Mark Twain, whom we do not ordinarily remember as a historical novelist, produced *The Prince and the Pauper* and *A Connecticut Yankee in King Arthur's Court.* One trait almost all of these had in common—as did most of the English historical novelists form Thackeray to Stevenson—is that they wrote for children, or wrote books which children took over and made their own. Teachers and scholars too commonly ignore the needs of children, forgetting that if they are to be attracted to the study of history their interests must be aroused and their sympathies enlisted, and forgetting that children want action, drama, adventure, heroes, and villains. These the historical novel offers them.

There are, in a broad way, two kinds of historical novels. There is the "costume piece"—the novel which quite deliberately seeks to recreate the past and to dramatize it; like a producer putting on an Elizabethan play, the author has to be sure to get all the "furniture" right—the clothing, the idiom, even the accent. Traditionally this kind of historical novel distorts history, leaving with the reader the impression that the past was a potpourri of fighting, derring-do, and nonstop romances by Scott or Dumas or Stevenson or John Buchan. But at its best this kind of historical fiction can be as faithful to history as a good many sober monographs, and can be, at the same time, great literature: Thackeray's *The Virginians,* Hawthorne's *Scarlet Letter,* Stendhal's *Charterhouse of Parma.* Tolstoy's *War and Peace,* Sigrid Undset's *Kristin Lavransdatter,* Thomas Mann's *Joseph and His Brethren,* and Lion Feuchtwanger's *Jew Süss* come readily to mind.

There is another and even more valuable genre of historical novel—the novel that is not deliberately "historical" at all, but that faithfully recreates a present which is or will be past, and which becomes, therefore, by virtue of its authenticity, a historical document. If we want to know what life was like in the comfortable upper classes of England during the Napoleonic wars we cannot do better than turn to the novels of Jane Austen—*Pride and Prejudice* or *Sense and Sensibility* or *Mansfield Park.* Is there anywhere a more faithful picture of Scotland during these same years than can be read in the salty pages of John Galt's *Annals of the Parish* or *The Entail*—unless it is possibly in the pages of Galt's contemporary, Susan Ferrier? Has anyone ever conjured up life in the London of the early nineteenth century more realistically than Dickens in *Nicholas Nickleby* or *Oliver Twist* or *Great Expectations*? What better way is there to understand the bourgeoisie of the Hansa towns than through Thomas Mann's *Buddenbrooks* or of French provincial towns than in the pages of *Madame Bovary*? Selma Lagerlöv has given us eighteenth century Sweden in the *Saga of Gösta Berling* and nineteenth century Sweden in *Jerusalem*; and Bjørnsen has done the same for Norway. Louis Couperus helps us to understand life in the crowded cities of the modern Netherlands, and if we turn to Denmark we have no better guide than Martin Andersen-Nexö whose *Pelle the Conqueror* and *Ditte Girl Alive* recreate Copenhagen as Dickens recreated London. No sociological treatises conjure up life in the provincial towns of industrial England more faithfully than Arnold Bennett's Five Towns stories—*Clayhanger* and *Old Wives' Tale* and others; no historian of the class system illuminates it better than do Galsworthy in the *Forsyte Saga* or Frank

Swinnerton in *Shops and Houses* or Virginia Woolf in *Day and Night*. Americans, too, can read their social history in works of fiction. William Dean Howells has some claim to be regarded as our most finished and comprehensive social historian: Howells, who gives us the placid life of Boston and of the hinterland of New England, the Vermont countryside, the Ohio frontier, and the turbulent life of New York City, and of the American abroad, and whose *Rise of Silas Lapham* is still in many ways the best portrayal of the American businessman in our literature. So it is with a host of others: the incomparable Henry James, foremost historian of the manners of the American leisure class and of the American expatriate, and most penetrating student of the American moral character; Edith Wharton with her sensitive feeling for the life of the upper classes of New York City and the Hudson Valley; Ellen Glasgow, who understood so fully what had happened to Virginia "after the War," and who explained it in a long series of novels carrying the history of Virginia from the Civil War to the twentieth century; Willa Cather, whose panels of life on the plains—*My Ántonia* and *O Pioneers* and *The Song of the Lark* and, best of all, *A Lost Lady*—are more realistic and penetrating than her formal historical novels. For a feeling of life on the farm in the years after the Civil War, and of the truth of the farm problem, we turn with confidence to Hamlin Garland's *Main Traveled Roads* or to Frank Norris' *The Octopus* or to Ole Rølvaag's wonderfully evocative *Giants in the Earth*, rather than to the formal histories; and the most penetrating accounts of the "revolt from the village" are, beyond doubt, such books as Sherwood Anderson's *Winesburg, Ohio* or Edgar Lee Masters' *Spoon River Anthology* or Sinclair Lewis' *Main Street*.

These observations apply with equal force to poetry and drama. Lord Tennyson's *Idylls of the King* and the plays of Henrik Ibsen are historical documents of the first order; read with insight and with sympathy they will illuminate the Victorian mind or the social history of Norway as brightly as any formal historical treatises on these subjects.

Writing History

So much for reading. What of the writing of history?

Let it be said at once that there is no mystery about writing history, nothing esoteric or cabalistic. There is no formula for historical writing. There are no special techniques or special requirements, except the technique of writing clearly and the requirements of honesty and common sense. It is useful to have special training, as it is useful to to have special training for almost anything you wish to do well—driving a car or cooking or painting—but special training is by no means essential, and most of the great historians have been innocent of formal training. Professional history is, indeed, a very recent affair—it came in with "technical history" in the nineteenth century—and, except in Germany, the near-monopoly of historical writing by academicians is even more recent. Almost all the great historians of the past were men involved in one way or another in public affairs—Thucydides, Livy, Tacitus, Plutarch and, in modern times, Bolingbroke, Voltaire, Hume, Macaulay, Bancroft, Guizot, Grundtvig. Most of them, too, were amateurs, at least in the sense that they were not professional teachers: thus in the United States Bancroft, Prescott, Motley, Parkman, and Henry Adams. The amateur tradition is now almost a thing of the past, but it lingers on in Europe more tenaciously than in America: witness the contributions of such public figures as Croce, Madariaga, Malraux, De Gaulle, George Lukacs, and Winston Churchill.

Integrity, industry, imagination, and common sense—these are the important, indeed the essential, requirements. They are by no means familiar commonplace qualities. The requirement of integrity is of course implacable, in history as in all other forms of scholarship or science, and there is no need to elaborate upon it. Yet here, too, it must be admitted that standards of "integrity" are not universal, and that honest men differ on the nature of truth in history as in all other realms of thought. Perhaps it is sufficient to say that the historian must be honest according to his lights; that he should never consciously distort his evidence, even by literary artistry; that he should be ever on guard against religious, racial, class or national preconceptions; that he should try to see every problem from all possible points of view; that he should search diligently for all the evidence, and not be content until he has exhausted the available resources; that he should always remember that he is not God and that final judgment is not entrusted to him.

The requirement of industry, too, is elementary and rigorous. You need not, perhaps, emulate the great historian of ancient Rome, Theodore Mommsen, who customarily worked eighteen hours a day and complained that on his wedding day he managed only twelve hours work, or that other German phenomenon, Leopold von Ranke, who kept working and writing well into his eighties, and who at the age of eighty-five launched a *History of the World,* seven volumes of which appeared in the next five years of his life. But, as with most things that are important, the writing of history requires patience, devotion, and indefatigable industry, much of it tiresome. You will have to accustom yourself to spending long hours and days tracking down some source which as often as not will prove quite useless, reading through newspapers or journals which as often as not yield only a scanty return, working patiently through ill-scrawled manuscripts in the hope, often vain, of hitting on something that is relevant to your inquiry, fighting your way stubbornly through the jungles of verbiage in the *Congressional Globe* or the *Reports* of royal commissions, or the decisions of courts. If you are going to come up with something that is new, original, fresh, and valuable, you cannot avoid these exercises; if you are not prepared for them, you will do well to abandon history for something less arduous.

As for imagination, that is in all likelihood something that cannot be cultivated; either you have it or you do not. If you do not have it you may be a worthy compiler of facts, a good analyst, a safe guide through the labyrinths of the past, but you will never be able to recreate that past, never set the blood coursing through the veins of your readers, or ideas tumbling over each other in their heads. As for "common sense"—alas it is by no means as common as the phrase implies. It is an all-inclusive term which embraces such disparate qualities as moderation, balance, judiciousness, critical intelligence, open-mindedness, tolerance, proportion, and good humor, and doubtless other qualities as well. Without it the most scholarly and interesting works misfire—for example, as with William Crosskey's two learned volumes designed to prove that the Founding Fathers meant something quite different from what they said and wrote, or Otto Eisenschiml's elaborate proof that Secretary Stanton master-minded the plot to assassinate Lincoln, or Charles Tansill's well-documented volumes designed to prove that Franklin Roosevelt instigated the Second World War, or—to take a more extreme example—those many volumes dedicated to the proposition that Lord Bacon or the Earl of Oxford or somebody else wrote the plays hitherto attributed to Shakespeare.

Let us turn, then, to some practical considerations in the writing of history: first, the choice of a subject. That seems almost too elementary a matter to justify comment, but alas it is not. Again and again otherwise sensible neophyte historians come a cropper when they select a subject for their investigation. Here is where common sense comes in. Your subject should not be too ambitious or too petty. It should not be too hackneyed or too esoteric. It should be something you can manage within the time you have available and the space. It should be something which has not been chewed up by generations of historians; at the same time it should not be something so strange and rare that it will be of interest only to you. Take care, too, that the materials you will need to use are not only available but available to you. Do not select some subject for which the materials are scanty and unreliable, or the essential documents inaccessible—some chapter in the history of the Secret Service, for example, or the CIA—or in the possession of a family which preserves them for its own purposes, or in the archives of Spain or Australia—unless indeed you happen to be bound for Spain or Australia. If you live in Montana do not select a subject which has to be studied in the files of eastern newspapers; if you live in New York City do not select a subject which has to be studied through materials scattered throughout a dozen western historical societies. If your command of languages is shaky, avoid subjects which require a knowledge of half a dozen foreign languages; if your eyesight is poor, avoid subjects which are to be studied in seventeenth or eighteenth century manuscripts or—for that matter—in the manuscripts of Horace Greeley or Charles Sumner or others whose handwriting was notoriously indecipherable.

All of this is purely negative—this elimination of subjects that do not lend themselves to orderly treatment. There is one affirmative consideration equally basic and imperative: select a subject the way you would select a friend or, perhaps, a spouse. It is something your are going to live with for a long time, perhaps for years; select therefore a good companion for the journey. Ideally you should find a subject which so interests and excites you that you cannot resist it. On the whole it is desirable to choose a subject which enlists your sympathy, though that is by no means essential. You can write effectively about the Massacre of St. Bartholomew even though you disapprove in principle of religious intolerance; you can write perspicaciously of Hilter without approving of Nazism; yet it is perhaps best to avoid the first if you are of Huguenot descent and the second if you are Jewish.

For biographical subjects it is particularly important to find a figure who enlists your sympathy as well as your interest. As you would not want to live intimately with someone you heartily disliked, so you will not want to live on terms of intimacy with some historical character whom you heartily dislike. There are examples of biographers who have disliked—or come to dislike—their subject: Froude certainly appeared to dislike Carlyle—though in fact he did not—and Lytton Strachey had no use for his Eminent Victorians, while Paxton Hibben scarcely tried to conceal his contempt for William Jennings Bryan. But these are exceptions. The best biographers confess admiration and sympathy for their subjects, and some of them deep personal affection—Boswell's famous biography of Dr. Johnson, for example, or William Dean Howells' tender interpretation, *My Mark Twain,* or George Otto Trevelyan's biography of his uncle, *Lord Macaulay.*

Once you have found a sympathetic subject, and ascertained that there is something new to be said about it and that the materials on which to base your study are ample and readily available, you can get started. And from now on common sense really does take charge.

Even here there are some practical observations that are relevant. The first is this: do not waste time and energy in what is amiably called "reading around" a subject. Reading around, or reading for background, is more often than not an excuse for not getting on with the job: it is pleasant; it is edifying—and it is inexhaustible. A chemist concerned with a specific problem does not stop to "read around" chemistry; a lawyer dealing with a specific case does not "read around" the law. Plunge into the subject itself; get your problem by the throat and grapple with it. The closer you come to it, and the deeper your understanding of it, the more surely you will become familiar with all the surrounding landscape. Gradually everything will fall into place. That, after all, is the natural way: you come only gradually to know the background of a friend, and even children do not fill in the background of parents and grandparents until they themselves have children. In short, start with the particular, not with the general; read deeply in the history of the particular, and you will find that the general takes care of itself.

A second practical rule is to begin almost at once collecting the essential materials for your essay or monograph and organizing them into some coherent pattern. Granted you do not really know what is "essential," or just what the pattern is to be; the sooner you get started, the sooner you will find answers to these questions. Do not think you have to read everything, take notes on everything, track down every reference, look at every piece of manuscript before you begin to write. The sooner you begin the better, for only as you write will you discover the lacunae in your knowledge and fill them.

There is a third practical consideration here that has to do with the compilation of your materials. For most purposes that means "taking notes"—that arduous and never-ending process which can, unless you are careful, become something of an opiate, a pleasant substitute for the real work of thinking and writing. Not long ago taking notes meant precisely that; the scholar painfully, and painstakingly, copied out mountains of passages which he hoped would one day prove useful, or hired someone to do it for him. Now all of that has changed; notetaking has been mechanized, like so many other things, and the happy researcher now sends materials off to be photostated, Xeroxed, or microfilmed—all much better than in the bad old days. Now you can get ten times as much copied, nay a hundred times as much; now you can be sure of accuracy; now you can save time and go everywhere and see everything! Fortunate scholars; now we may expect them all to write twice as much as any former generation. How odd that they write only half as much!

We are all immensely indebted to modern techniques of mechanical reproduction, but do not be carried away by them to the point where you think that history itself has become mechanized. It is all very well to have machines do your copying for you, but remember that they cannot think for you. Something is to be said for doing things yourself—even for copying documents yourself. The great literary historian Van Wyck Brooks, author of the most interesting of literary histories of America, did all his own copying and, what is more, did it all by hand. He could, of course, have employed copyists or bought himself a copying machine. He preferred to do his own work because he knew what every scholar comes to know: that if you copy things yourself, you remember them. He knew, too, another important lesson: that the by-product of copying is often more important than the product, namely the ideas you get as you go. No machine can get those ideas for you, and there is no substitute for the inspiration which comes from your own direct, fresh, and uncomplicated relation with your materials.

When it comes to writing history, keep in mind that there are almost as many ways of writing as there are historians. There is no formula; you will have to find your own formula. There is no pattern; you will have to work out your own pattern. But this is not to suggest that there are no models. There are models by the score. You will doubtless be influenced by them, just as a painter is influenced by Rembrandt or Goya, Whistler or Picasso. That does not mean that you can successfully adopt for your own the lordly style of a Gibbon, the rhetorical style of a Carlyle, the balanced cadences of a Macaulay, the strong masculine style of a Mahan, the brilliant style of a Parrington, the epigrammatic style of a Phillip Guedalla, the allusive style of a Denis Brogan, the intimate style of a Paul Hazard. All of these are available, but in writing, as in other matters, the style reflects the person and your style must reflect you.

But style is not a single or a static thing; you will want to vary your style, to adapt it to the subject matter. You would not think of using the same pattern of organization, the same style of presentation, for all subjects, any more than you would clothe all men and women alike at all times. A style suitable, let us say, to a history of the Tariff of 1890 is not a good style for a history of the conquest of Peru or for a biography of Herman Melville. Each subject makes its own claim upon you; each one demands individual treatment. Thomas Beer, for example—he was a novelist as well as a historian—used very different styles in his biography of *Stephen Crane* and his essay on *The Mauve Decade;* John Morley varied his style to suit the different requirements of *Voltaire* and of *Gladstone;* Henry Adams had one style for the *History* and a quite different one for the *Education,* more subtle, more allusive, though not more brilliant.

four

Some Problems of History

Limitations on the Historian

"The historian," writes Veronica Wedgwood, "ought to be the humblest of men; he is faced a dozen times a day with the evidence of his own ignorance; he is perpetually confronted with his own humiliating inability to interpret his material correctly; he is, in a sense that no other writer is, in bondage to that material." In bondage! Most sophisticated historians would readily agree with this. They are ever conscious of the limitations and handicaps under which they work and of the temptations and dangers to which they are exposed. But the public tends to overlook these limitations, and some historians are even innocent enough, or brash enough, to gloss over the difficulties inherent in their profession.

History is in fact far more complex and disorderly than the amateur suspects. To most laypeople it is all simple and straightforward. What is it that you want to know? Is it the writing of the Magna Carta, the consolidation of Germany under Bismarck, the triumph of Communism in China? Get your facts; put them together in some sensible order. And presto! There is your history. The great historian Henry Adams has made the classic observation on this notion of history. "He had even published a dozen volumes of American history," he recalled, "for no other purpose than to satisfy himself whether, by the severest process of stating, with the least possible comment, such facts as seemed sure in such order as seemed rigorously consequent, he could fix for a familiar moment a necessary sequence of human movement." The result, he confessed, was failure. "Where he saw sequence other men saw something quite different, and no one saw the same unit of measure," and he concluded that "the sequence of men led to nothing and that the sequence of their society could lead no further, while the mere sequence of time was artificial, and the sequence of thought was chaos."[1] So he abandoned history altogether and asserted, somewhat perversely, that any nine pages of his novel, *Esther,* were worth more than the nine volumes of his *History.* Posterity does not agree with this verdict, but that is another matter.

What then, are some of these limitations which have discouraged so many historians, and which, Wedgwood admonished us, should induce humility?

First, there are the many and sobering limitations on historical materials. There is, for example, the role of fortuity. The chemist or biologist can command whatever materials he needs for experiments, but the historian works with what happens to come to hand. What we are permitted "to know" is not only but a small part of "what happened in history," but it is a miscellany which has come to us in large part by chance rather than by choice. What we can see of history is far less than what we can see of the iceberg; most of it, too, is buried and forever lost. It is lost because it was never compiled; it is lost because of the erosion of time — fire and water and weather and carelessness; it is lost because it was deliberately destroyed. How do we know that what has come down to us is either the most important or the most authentic representation of any chapter of past history?

Another limitation is that of distortion; the record of the past, as we have it, is monstrously lopsided. Thus we know a great deal of the history of some European peoples, and because this record is available we confuse it with history and write as if it embraced the whole of the past. It is not merely that the records for most non-European societies are nonexistent or lost—the African, for example, or the American Indian or the Carthagenian—but that even where records are available—in China or in India, for example—Western historians have not used them. This is easy to understand, but we should not call what we choose to interest ourselves in history, and formulate broad, even universal, generalizations on the basis of such fragmentary and arbitrary evidence.

The very fact that history is based so largely on the written record introduces a note of unbalance and distorts our view. For what it inevitably means is that we exaggerate the role of the written record and of those peoples who did keep records at the expense of those who did not, or whose records are fitful and uninformative. Almost every historian has an unconscious bias in favor of the literary history-conscious, western European, and against the others: in favor of the Jews and against the Babylonians, in favor of the Greeks and against the Persians, in favor of the Romans and against the "barbarians." Even in highly sophisticated societies such as our own we must acknowledge a distortion induced by the charms of the written record. How much of American history has been colored by the fact that New Englanders have been more assiduous in keeping records and more effective in presenting them than, let us say, Virginians or Carolinians; Jamestown came before Plymouth, but every schoolchild knows, from poetry, fiction, and painting as well as from history, the story of the Pilgrims and the Puritans. The slave-owner was literate and articulate, the black slave illiterate and inarticulate; it was, until recently, the slave-owner's version of slavery which came down to us and which was widely accepted as history.

The seduction, or tyranny, of the written record introduces another element of distortion, namely, that what attracts the record-keeper and the historian is the dramatic, the spectacular, the bizarre, and the catastrophic. This has always been true, and it remains true today, as reference to any daily newspaper will make clear. The monkish chroniclers who bequeathed us so many records did not customarily record the daily routine of life, but only events which they considered out of the ordinary or miraculous: comets and earthquakes and plagues and wars; and millions of families have endorsed this view of history by recording in their family Bibles only births, marriages, and deaths. The historian too is attracted by whatever is dramatic or unusual or romantic; he or she writes the annals of the rich and the great; for the annals of the poor, as we know, are short and simple. How natural it is for us, how inevitable perhaps, to believe that history is, by its very nature, the record of what is dramatic and astonishing. A great statesman, a soldier, an explorer, we say "makes history"; or a particular people at a particular time—the Athenians of the fifth century B. C., or the French during their Revolution, "make history." This is, of course, nonsense; everybody makes history all the time, the slave as well as the master, the South Sea Islander as well as the Parisian. What we mean is that these people make the kind of history that appeals to us, that we happen to know about, and that we like to write about; it follows very easily that what appeals to us and what we write about is history.

Closely associated with the enchantment of the dramatic is the spell of the familiar. So accustomed are we to the formal patterns of history that it requires a convulsive effort for us to remember that these are not history's patterns, but ours. We have already considered the dangers latent in familiar chronological and regional patterns—the habit of dividing history into neat packets labeled Ancient, Medieval, and Modern, or of carving up American history into Colonial, Revolutionary, Middle Period, and so forth. There is a further refinement on these divisions which is even more artificial, the habit of forcing history into the straitjackets of monarchical or presidential patterns. Thus we write of the Age of Louis XIV or of Napoleon, of the Jeffersonian era, or the era of Franklin D. Roosevelt.

Of all patterns which we have imposed upon history, it is the national which is the most powerful and the most pervasive, and perhaps the most mischievous. The limitations which nationalism imposes upon history go far beyond those of providing convenient but misleading patterns; we shall deal at greater length with these further limitations.

The parochialism of nationalism or of race is familiar, and most of us try to guard against it. We are less aware of and more vulnerable to another form of parochialism, the parochialism of time.

Present-mindedness is, perhaps, the most intractable of all the limitations on history—our instinctive habit of looking at the past through our own eyes, judging it by our own standards, recreating it in our own words, or reading back into the language of the past our own meanings, assuming that whatever happened, happened in some "past" and forgetting that every past was once a present. It is probable that we are, to a large degree, helpless in this matter; try as we will we cannot "think ourselves back into a twilight," to use Maitland's wonderful phrase. We cannot really put ourselves inside the minds, or skins, of Cyrus or Brutus or Joan of Arc or the Indian chief Pontiac. That we do try is a tribute to the rigor of our historical conscience, and a few great histories and biographies are monuments to the fact that we are not always unsuccessful, though in the nature of the case we are not permitted to know even this. But the difficulty of present-mindedness is really deeper. It is that we almost instinctively assume that the past was made just for us, that it is interesting only insofar as it caters to our current interests, and significant only when it has ostentatious consequences for us. How easily we fall into what might be called the fallacy of "quaintness"—the fallacy of supposing that medieval people were medieval in their own eyes as well, or that Renaissance Man betrays us if he does not live up to our notion of what he should be, or that the Forefathers knew that they were Forefathers. How hard it is for us to realize that the past was as real to those who lived in it as the present is to us and that they no more lived for our edification than we live for the edification of distant future generations.

There is another danger implicit in present-mindedness, one, again, which we cannot, in the nature of things, escape, but against which we must everlastingly guard ourselves. That is what we may call the danger of the *fait accompli.* We know what happened in history and because we know it, we can never look back upon it with the eyes of innocence. We know that the Athenian expedition to Syracuse is going to fail; that Rome will humble Carthage, and the Roman Republic change into an empire; that the Moslems will eventually be driven out of western Europe, and that Christianity will triumph; that it is the English who will win the struggle for the American continent; that no matter how dark the outlook Washington will lead his ragged army to victory at Yorktown; that no matter how glittering the prospects, Robert E. Lee is headed for Appomattox. We are, all of us, in the position of the reader of mystery stories who reads the last chapter first. But we should remember that we do not know how our own history is going to come out, and neither did earlier generations.

Our inability to divorce ourselves from knowing how history is going to come out almost guarantees that our view of the past will be astigmatic. We inevitably read back into the past what we know occurred, and adopt a *post hoc propter hoc* attitude toward history. As Rome is bound to fall to the barbarian invaders, we find explanations of that fall in the corruption and immorality of public life; as Britain is doomed to lose her American colonies, we accept Tom Paine's observation that it is absurd for a continent to belong to an island; as the Confederacy is predestined to defeat, we confidently find the causes of that defeat. But if we adopt these postions, we render ourselves incapable of understanding the past in its own terms. As David Donald has said, historians are camp-followers of victorious armies. Knowing which side is going to win—the Romans, Christianity, the Union, the Atlantic powers—they instinctively ally themselves with the winning side; they look for explanations of what triumphed and ignore the evidence on the other side. Some of them see the hand of God, or of Progress or of Evolution, in whatever triumphed and whatever failed.

Nothing, surely, is more fatal to the integrity of historical investigation than the doctrine of inevitability implicit in this attitude. For if whatever happened in history was inevitable, whether because it expressed the will of God or the force of evolution or of progress, then there is little point in conducting any investigation whatsoever into the causes or the consequences of things. *Felix qui potuit rorum cognascere causas,* but if the causes of things are predestined, there is no happiness, and no value either. As Charles A. Beard warned us:

> If all human affairs were reduced to law, to a kind of terrestrial mechanics, a chief end of
> the quest, that is, human control over human occurrences and actions, would itself

become meaningless. Should mankind discover the law of its total historical unfolding, then it would be imprisoned in its own fate, and powerless to change it; the past, present and future would be revealed as fixed and beyond the reach of human choice and will. Men and women would be chained to their destinies as the stars and tides are to their routine. [2]

But, as far as we know, the course of history is not predestined. Life has always been, as it is now, "a roar of bargain and of battle," and the intellectual challenge to understand the past is no less compelling than the challenge to understand the present and the future. There is, to be sure, one sobering difference here. If we understand the present we may be able to command it, but there is no way by which we can command the past.

The Trouble with Facts

These are some of the limitations on the historian. But there are limitations inherent in the facts of history as well.

Poor, despised facts, they have a hard time. Nobody believes in them; nobody has any faith in them. With almost a single voice historians say that there are no facts, none that can be relied upon anyway; there are only some agreed-on assumptions which we choose to call facts so we can get on with the job. But do not be misled by them, do not take them seriously, or they will betray you. Facts are subjective; they exist in the mind of the historian, and they change their character with each historian. The facts of the Franco-Prussian War are one thing to a French historian, another to a German; the facts about the creation of the state of Israel read very differently in the eyes of Jews and Arabs. Facts are like the Cheshire cat in *Alice in Wonderland;* as we look at them they fade away, all but the grin.

What is the trouble with facts?

First, a paradox. There are too few facts, and there are too many. There are far too few facts about immense areas of past history. How little we know, after all, about most of humankind—about the people of Asia, of Africa, of pre-Columbian America; how little we know about lost people like the Carthaginians and the Etruscans, the early Celts and the Basques. How little we know about the remote past, as contrasted with the recent past. How do we dare reconstruct the ancient world with any assurance, when our knowledge is confined to small areas around the Mediterranean? Yet we confidently call this ancient history. How can we write with any assurance about the history of the American continents when—except for what ethnology and archeology may tell us—our knowledge embraces only five centuries out of a possible twenty-five thousand years? How little we know—even in modern times—of the lives of the poor, of those vast majorities of each generation about whom we have no reliable facts.

And, at the other end of the spectrum, we know almost too much about the modern history of the West—the United States, Britain, France, Germany, and Italy in the nineteenth or twentieth centuries. We are overwhelmed by mountains of evidence; it accumulates faster than even computers can record it, and we still have to process the material from the computers. We do not and cannot have all the facts about the Second World War, but it is safe to conjecture that historians will never get through the miles of filing cases of historical records now resting in warehouses throughout the country. Inevitably our vision of the past is distorted by this dispro-portion in our evidence; inevitably we translate this disproportion into historical distortion.

We have already noted the role of caprice and fortuity in the historical record, and the influence of modern-mindedness and of subjectivity. There are still further limitations on "facts." There is, for example, the elementary consideration that we can rarely attain factual accuracy about the past, even about the recent past. The uninitiated take factual accuracy for granted in history as they take it for granted in chemistry or physics, but as soon as they try to reconstruct any chapter of past history they speedily discover that accuracy is unattainable. The science of statistics is new, and even such statistics as we have are rarely reliable. We do not know such fundamental things as the populations or the birth and death rates of ancient peoples; we do not know the numbers in armies or in battles, or the casualties in war. We do not know the value or the volume of farm production or of domestic industries or of trade. Even in modern history, statistics often fail us: we do not and probably cannot know with any accuracy the number of soldiers in the Union or the Confed-erate armies or the losses or the cost of the war; the ascertainable "facts" do not go very far in explaining why Britain did not intervene on the side of the Confederacy. Even so apparently elementary a matter as the total acreage of public lands granted by state and federal governments to American railroads has long been and still is a matter of conjecture and debate. On these, and a hundred other important questions of history, we can only make educated guesses.

There are, to be sure, some matters about which we can be accurate and certain, but alas, these turn out to be matters of no great importance. We can be accurate about the succession of American presidents, or of the kings of England or France, and we prefer a historian who knows that Buchanan succeeded Pierce, and not the other way around, and who can list the Richards and the Henrys, the Philips and the Louis in their proper order. This is too elementary to be helpful. We can be accurate about the dates of the Buchanan administration, but not about Buchanan's role in the coming of the Civil War; we can be accurate about the dates for Louis XVI, but there is no agreement on his contribution to the breakdown of the *ancien régime*.

Finally, the facts of history turn out to be not hard and objective but impalpable and subjective. Ranke and his successors taught us to rely on documents for our history; the documents, they were confident, would speak for themselves. Alas, they do not speak for themselves. They speak, rather, for us, and with a hundred different voices, usually raucous and clashing. They tell us not what actually happened but, more often than not, what we want to hear. Take, for example, the two most famous documents of American history—the Declaration of Independence and the federal Constitution. Even the textual history of the Declaration is an intricate affair, but look aside from the textual history to the political and philosophical. Here are the immortal words—their immortality, note, not inherent, but conferred upon them by later generations— what do they mean? What did Jefferson and the members of the Continental Congress mean when he wrote, and they endorsed, the statement that "all men are created equal"? What did he mean when he wrote, what did they mean when they endorsed, the sentiment that the "pursuit of happiness" is an unalienable right?

No two people read quite the same thing into these words. Certainly the genera-tion of Thomas Jefferson (even the term *generation* is an artificial one, and if we accept Jefferson's own calculation of a generation as twenty years, he belonged to four!) and our own generation read different meanings into terms like *equality* and *happiness.* Certainly, too, in our own day, men and women read different meanings into the word *happiness,* and northerners and southerners, whites and blacks, read different meanings into the term *equality.* It requires a lifetime of study to understand these esoteric words, and after a lifetime of study different historians come up with very different explanations. Clearly this famous document does not speak for itself.

Contemplate, then, the Constitution of the United States, a document of some six thousand carefully chosen words, simple, lucid, logical. Does the Constitution speak for itself? Clearly it does not; if it did we should not need the 375 volumes of Supreme Court *Reports* to explain and interpret it; nor would learned and upright judges on the Supreme Court so frequently disagree about the meaning of such phrases as "commerce among the several states," "the executive power," "impair the obligation of contracts," "common defense and general welfare," "necessary and proper," and "due process of law."

Or take another kind of document: a painting. Does the meaning of the painting inhere in the painting itself? Not entirely. You can look at it and see a great deal which you have missed; an art historian or art critic can look at it through the eyes of history and see many things which escape the rest of us and some, perhaps, which were not in the mind of the artist when he painted the picture.

Take, for example, the various paintings by Poussin on the theme *Et in Arcadia Ego,* which Edwin Panofsky has dealt with in a fascinating essay on that subject. To the onlooker it is a simple matter—shepherds and maidens stumbling on a tomb with that touching inscription are struck into sober contemplation by the realization that others before them had lived in Arcadia and now were dead and gone. But is that really what the paintings mean, or what the phrase and the concept originally meant? Not at all, says Panofsky. What they mean is not "I too have lived in Arcadia," but "Death, too, is in Arcadia." That reverses the moral of the pictures completely; it is no longer a reminder that every generation has known happiness, but a reminder that death is ever present, even in Arcadia. But hold, it is not that simple, either, for eighteenth-century painters did in fact reverse the original meaning. Unwilling to contemplate the presence of death in Arcadia, they turned the whole thing into a pastoral scene, one designed to show that generation was linked to generation by happiness, not by death.

Contemplate another, and more familiar, artistic document: Emanuel Leutze's painting of "Washington Crossing the Delaware." Clearly this is not a contemporary record: there were no artists present to record that famous crossing. It was painted three-quarters of a century after the event; the river was the Rhine, not the Delaware, and Washington was Worthington Whittredge, a young American artist studying in Düsseldorf. The scene itself was a product of Leutze's romantic imagination. If Washington had stood up in that rowboat he would have fallen overboard; the flag was quite incorrect; and as the crossing was made before dawn of a winter night, neither Washington nor the sailors who rowed him would have been visible in the dark. But all that was of no importance. The painting had a life of its own. It was accepted with rapture as an authentic representation; it made its way at once into the minds and hearts of the American people; it has come to be, for all practical purposes, the authentic representation of the historic event. If it does not reproduce a historical fact it is, itself, a historical fact.

A document, then, may mean many things. Its meaning is to be understood in the light of its own contemporary history; it is to be understood in the light of the reason, temperament, and prejudices of the historian who uses it; it is to be arrived at and interpreted through the symbolism it communicates. Even that is not the end of it. For the historian has to communicate with each individual reader, and each one will read the document or the analysis in his or her own way, just as each individual looks at a Whistler painting or listens to a Mozart sonata in his or her own way.

The facts of history are fragmentary, elusive, and subjective. But that is true of most of these studies which engage the minds and the passions of human beings— art and letters, morals and ethics, even law and politics, as every judge and statesman knows. We must not expect things to be easier for the historian than they are for those many others who try somehow to reconcile the heritage of the past—its laws and principles and monuments—with the imaginations, the passions, the emotions, and the facts of their own time.

Yet though we admit the limitations and difficulties of history, item by item, if we take them too hard, we will find ourselves out of a job. If the limitations really are so severe, and the facts really are so elusive, we may be forced to give up history altogether. If we are to get on with the job, we must agree upon some kind of factual foundation or framework for our histories, if only that Washington was in fact the first President of the United States or that the United States did in fact fight a war with Mexico which brought it Texas and California or that Lincoln was in fact assassinated. For, treacherous as they no doubt are, facts are like syntax and grammar; we need them as a framework and a mechanism if we are to make ourselves clear. There is nothing sacred about grammar, and a wide latitude is permitted in its usage, but if we are perpetually to stop and question the authority of our grammar we will never finish what we are saying or writing.

Historians have, after all, surmounted the difficulties that crowd about them, and given us famous and affluent histories. Gibbon was aware of the difficulties, and Macaulay, Ranke, and Mommsen, Maitland and Holdsworth, Parkman and Henry Adams; yet all of them managed to write histories which have enlarged the thoughts and lifted the spirits of generations of people.

Interpretation—and Bias

Let us admit at once that history is neither scientific nor mechanical, that the historian is human and therefore fallible, and that the ideal history, completely objective and dispassionate, is an illusion. There is bias in the choice of a subject, bias in the selection of material, bias in its organization and presentation, and, inevitably, bias in its interpretation. Consciously, or unconsciously, all historians are biased: they are creatures of their time, their race, their faith, their class, their country—creatures, and even prisoners.

Most historians strive courageously to avoid bias and achieve objectivity when they teach or write history, but there have always been some who out of defiance, or out of acquiescence to the inevitable, have accepted the fact of bias and tried to make a virtue of it. The famous German historian Heinrich von Treitschke represents the first attitude. Writing in 1865, he asserted that a "bloodless objectivity which does not say on which side is the narrator's heart, is the exact opposite of the true historical sense," and in his own multivolumed *History of Germany in the Nineteenth Century* he left no one in doubt about what side his heart was on, or his mind and his temper either. The American Charles A. Beard represents the second attitude. "Any selection and arrangement of facts," he said in his address on "History as an Act of Faith," "pertaining to any large area of History, either local or world, race or class, is controlled inexorably by the frame of reference in the mind of the selector or arranger." As long as this was true, he concluded, it was only honorable for the historian frankly to acknowledge his "frame of reference" — that is, his bias. And, as history is, inevitably, an instrument of propaganda, said Beard, let us take care that it is propaganda for good causes, for peace and progress, for justice and truth, and not for bad.

Pity the poor historian. He is the victim, the prisoner, of circumstances, of nature and of human nature. Even St. Anthony was not exposed to so many temptations. Is he a modern man: then how will he ever understand medieval man? Is he a European: can he ever really understand and do justice to the world of Asia and of Africa — or even of America? Is he a white man: can he really understand the Third World peoples who constitute three-quarters of the human race? Is he a Christian: can he do justice to those he has learned to designate pagans or heathens? Is he a Catholic: can he be fair to Protestants? Is he a Protestant: can he be fair to the Papacy and the Inquisition? Is he — and he almost certainly is — a member of the middle or the upper classes, literate and educated: can he really understand the point of view of the workingperson and the peasant? Can a liberal like Macaulay do justice to the Stuarts? Can a Marxist like Albert Mathiez do justice to the ancien régime — or even to the Gironde? Can a Republican like Albert Beveridge understand Jefferson or a Democrat like Claude Bowers understand Hamilton or a New Dealer like Arthur Schlesinger, Jr., be fair to Herbert Hoover? Can a Georgia gentleman like Ulrich B. Phillips ever really understand slavery? Can a black Marxist like W. E. B. Du Bois write dispassionately of slaveholders or of southern Bourbons? Can an Englishman or an Irishman, a German or a Frenchman be expected to emancipate himself from national predilections and write history that gives no hint of national affiliations or loyalties?

It was the hope of Lord Acton that a new generation of historians could answer all these questions in the affirmative. When, in 1896, he launched the cooperative Cambridge Modern History, he told potential contributors that "we shall avoid the needless utterance of opinion or service of a cause. Contributors will understand that our Waterloo must satisfy French and English, Germans and Dutch alike; that nobody can tell, without examining the list of authors, where the Bishop of Oxford laid down the pen and whether Fairbairn or Gasquet, Liebermann or Harrison took it up." But few historians have ever really managed to live up to these austere standards, and it doubtful whether Acton did himself.

It is easy enough to discern bias in history, easy enough to recognize a great deal of what passes for history as propaganda of varying degrees of subtlety. Much of this propaganda does not rise to the dignity of history — the histories, put out by Nazi historians, designed to prove the superiority of the Aryan race and the virtue of Hitlerian Germany; the "new-think" put out by Communist historians to justify every turn and twist of Communist policy. But we should remember, too, that some of the most influential works of history have been propaganda: Clarendon's classic History of the Rebellion, for example, or the Abbé Raynal's Philosophical History of the Indies — an "instrument of war" against the Church — or Frederic Masson's adulatory but learned biography of Napoleon, or Henry Wilson's *Rise and Fall of the Slave Power in America.* In our own day we can readily discern elements of propaganda, or partisanship, in such major works as Charles A. Beard's studies of American foreign policy between the wars or Parrington's brilliant *Main Currents of American Thought* or Winston Churchill's *World Crisis,* but we do not really think the worse of them for that.

Actually partisanship often adds zest to historical writing; for partisanship is an expression of interest and excitement and passion, and these can stir the reader as judiciousness might not. Certainly Macaulay lives, while Stubbs and Gardiner are read only by the specialists; Motley's thrilling story of the *Rise of the Dutch Republic* has inspired generations of readers with enthusiasm for liberty and detestation of tyranny which cannot be wholly misguided; Parrington, for all his faults, excites an interest in American literature that no other historian or critic has been able to equal; Winston Churchill's splendid tributes to English courage had consequences to history that no other histories of this century could match. As that immaculate historian Lord Acton himself observed, "the strongest and most impressive personalities... project their own broad shadows upon their pages. This is a practice proper to great men, and a great man may be worth several immaculate historians."

Let us, then, not be too distressed that history is unscientific, partisan, and hopelessly subjective; that it lends itself so readily to misrepresentation and even to propaganda; that it reflects, for better or for worse, the personality, the prejudices, the idiosyncrasies of historians. The subjectivity is inevitable; the partisanship is regrettable, but has compensations; the propaganda usually takes care of itself, for it carries with it a kind of built-in discount; the idiosyncrasy is almost always interesting. And let us remember, too, that nothing which deals with human beings can approach scientific objectivity, that there is no wholly impartial justice, no wholly impartial political, economic, or social theory, no impartial education.

There is one bias, one prejudice, one obsession, so pervasive and so powerful that it deserves special consideration: nationalism. History, which should be the most cosmopolitan of studies, most catholic in its sympathies, most ecumenical in its interests, has, in the past century and a half, become an instrument of nationalism.

Nationalism is, no doubt, the most powerful force in modern history, and it is scarcely surprising that it should have captured historiography and enslaved historians. Historians no longer write in a universal language—Latin, for example, or, in the eighteenth century, French—but in the national vernacular; they adapt their history to a national framework, depend on national archives and similar sources for materials, and almost inevitably express a national point of view. In the eighteenth century the ardors of nationalism were moderated by rationalism and cosmopolitanism, and if such books as Hume's *England,* Robertson's *Scotland,* or Müller's *Switzerland* threw history a bit out of focus, they did no serious violence to historical truth. Very different was the nationalist history which came in, as on flood tide, with the French Revolution and Napoleon, and with modern, chauvinistic nationalism. The new history reflected national interests, prejudices, and passions or, worse, stimulated them. It is a far cry from the cool rationalism of Robertson's *Scotland* to the romantic lyricism of Michelet's *France,* the savage chauvinism of Treitschke's *Germany,* the patriotic passion of Francis Palacky's *History of the Bohemian People,* or even the ardent enthusiasm of George Bancroft's *History of the United States.*

Nationalism, as we know it, is both recent and parochial. It was invented by western Europeans—British, French, Germans—and has flourished for less than 200 years. For historians to confuse it with universal history or—as some do—with the cosmic system, to read into it absolute values and absolute virtues, to identify themselves—and truth—passionately with one nation rather than another, is to betray history itself. It is to violate what should be the historical categorical imperative: never to subordinate the whole to the part, the permanent to the transient, the end to the means.

Overt bias, such as that which responds to nationalism, is easy to detect and not difficult to discount. There is a more subtle form of bias which is implicit in and all but inextricable from that present-mindedness which we considered earlier. This is sometimes called the problem of *nunc pro tunc:* the now for the then, the present for the past. What point of view should the historian adopt when he or she deals with the past, or with societies and civilizations very different from his or her own? Should historians maintain their own standards and values, or should they try to adopt the standards and values of the peoples and the age with which they are concerned?

At first glance this problem seems easy enough: the right and proper thing to do is to adopt the measure and the standards of the era and the people we are trying to understand and to explain. How absurd, after all, to judge the Persians, or even the Egyptians or the Greeks, by the standards of modern England: how absurd to judge the American Indian by the standards of eighteenth-century Europe; how misguided to apply our own artistic standards to ancient China or India, our intellectual and scientific standards to the Middle Ages. No, let us rather enter into the minds and the spirits of the people we are studying. So said Ranke, and all those who, after him, developed what it is fashionable to call historicism. Let us so immerse ourselves in the past that we can see with their eyes, hear with their ears, think as they thought, and feel as they must have felt: only by emancipating ourselves from the present and re-entering into the past can we be true to history; only by this renunciation of our own personalities can we hope to recover the character of the past.

This ideal was hopefully advanced in a biography of the "Great American Preacher" Theodore Parker:

> I have tried to know and to feel what Parker and his friends knew and felt, to accept the limitations of their minds, and, perhaps, of their characters. I have tried to see men and measures with Parker's eyes, to react to the events of the time as he did, or as I think that he did. I have permitted Parker to act as he chose to act, to render such judgment as he wished to make, to love those friends whom he did love, and to disparage those persons whom he disliked, whether he was wise in all this, or unwise. Where he was vain I have not sought to rebuke his vanity, where he was inconsistent I have not thought it necessary to remark his inconsistency, where he was ungenerous I have not taken him to task, where he was violent I have not tried to abate his violence, where he was mistaken I have not attempted to set him right; all of these things he confessed in his own words and actions and they appear without my intervention. [3]

Douglas Freeman, the distinguished biographer of Robert E. Lee, attempted to achieve this goal by the somewhat mechanical method of limiting himself, quite rigorously, to knowing only what Lee knew, and writing entirely within that framework of knowledge or of ignorance. Still another method of recreating the past is that used by two masters of intellectual history, the American, Van Wyck Brooks, and the Frenchman, Paul Hazard; it is the technique of literary intimacy. Here is Hazard describing the adventurers of the eighteenth century:

> In those days no one would stop in one place. Here was Montesquieu, off on the search for political constitutions; Diderot, after holding out against the idea for a long time, at length made the journey to Russia. Then, one fine day, the youthful Goldsmith resolves to set out for the Continent, and set out he does, without a penny to his name, with no one to fall back on in case of need, and with no definite itinerary in view. However, off he goes, playing his flute at cottage doors in the hope of getting, maybe, a bowl of soup or a shake-down in a barn. Holberg says good-bye to Denmark, and takes to the road, relying on his fine voice, as Goldsmith on his flute-playing, to get him along. On he goes, from country to country, learns French in Paris, and teaches it at Oxford. He was not a man to be baulked by trifles. All these inquiring gentlemen, indeed, are as mobile as can be, and they are never satisfied, they've never seen enough. [4]

This is all admirable, but does it really enable us to recapture the past? We may believe that we can think as Theodore Parker thought, or know only what General Lee knew, or live and feel with the *philosophes,* but perhaps we delude ourselves.

For when we turn to the past and use the literature or the monuments of the past as a means of entering its mind and spirit, how do we know that we have chosen correctly? The *philosophes* whom Hazard celebrates left an immense and entrancing literature, but did they really speak for France or for Germany in the eighteenth century? The abolitionists of New England were incomparably articulate, but they were few in number and of feeble influence; they speak for themselves, to be sure, but do they speak for New England? We can, of course, confine ourselves to single individuals; we can spend a lifetime immersing ourselves in the writings of Jefferson or Edmund Burke or Napoleon until we come, at last, to think as these men thought. Ah, but do we? How does it happen that men and women who have in fact spent a lifetime with these great figures come up with such different reports?

We can doubtless do quite well in understanding the past—where the literature is voluminous, where the society is familiar, and where the past is recent. But what shall we say of the attempt to enter into the minds and thoughts of a distant or unfamiliar past—of the Spartans, for example, who differed so profoundly from the Athenians; of the Aztecs or the Incas whose records are fragmentary; of the Danes who invaded and harried England in the ninth century? Perhaps we can manage to understand Jefferson or Burke; can we manage to understand the Persian Cyrus or Eric the Red?

There are many things to be said for accepting our limitations and looking at the past through the eyes of the present, but this is the most persuasive: no matter how hard we try, that is what we do anyway. We see the past through our own eyes, translate its language into our own, find interesting the things that interest us, and find significant the events that have had consequences for us. All this helps explain why each generation rewrites the history of the past: the view depends upon the point of view.

Consider, for example, the vicissitudes of the interpretation of Reconstruction by American historians.

Only half a century ago almost all students learned that after Appomattox the North imposed upon the stricken South a Punic peace, and they learned, too, that almost everything that happened—or failed to happen—thereafter could be blamed on the sins of Reconstruction. Through the tears that streamed from our sympathetic eyes we read that the federal government confiscated two billion dollars worth of slave property, that it imposed military rule upon the helpless South, that it forced—or tried to force—black equality upon a proud people long before the black was ready for equality or for anything; that it tolerated maladministration and corruption such as had never been known before in American history. In fact that generation of historians—the generation that ruled the roost during the first third of the twentieth century—was so ashamed of what the nation had done to the South that it almost apologized for fighting and winning the Civil War. Lee was the hero, not Grant, Confederate gray the stylish uniform, not Union blue, and everyone sang "Dixie Land." But now we look back on Reconstruction through very different eyes—or very different historical glasses. Now we regard it from the point of view of a generation that has lived through a war incomparably more savage and more destructive than the Civil War, and through peacemaking incomparably more im- placable than any that came in 1865. We have lost some of that innocence which still survived through the Victorian Age and into the new century, and lost our capacity to be surprised at ruthlessness, harshness, vindictiveness. Now when we look back at the American Civil War and Reconstruction it is with eyes that have seen what happened to the White Russians when the Bolsheviks won out; what happened to the Spanish Loyalists when Franco won out; what happened to the rebels first against Batista and then against Castro in Cuba; what happened to those desperate officers who tried to overthrow Hitler in 1944. And when we look at Reconstruction not from a provincial American but from a world point of view we see that in all modern history no civil war was concluded with so little blood-letting or vindictive- ness, and that in all modern history there is no example of magnanimity to compare with that which Lincoln and the national government displayed toward the defeated rebels. Now instead of writing the history of Reconstruction in terms of a Punic peace, we say rather that it was a magnanimous peace; instead of emphasizing the loss to slave-holders we emphasize the victory for black slaves; instead of deploring the establishment of military rule in the South we are astonished that the civil authority was so speedily restored and that the South was back in the Union—and even running it—within a few years. Instead of lamenting the fate of Jefferson Davis, languishing in prison for over a year, we note that after the greatest civil war of the century not one rebel lost his life, not one was proscribed, except briefly. And now, too, we reexamine—once again—the role of President Andrew Johnson, who first excited our reprobation and then our sympathies, and of the Radicals, who for a time excited our admiration, and then our contempt. We reexamine these in the light of recent developments in the position of the black in American life, and ask whether the Radical program might not have set the black question on the way to solution instead of leaving it for us to grapple with a century later. It would be presumptuous to say which of these points of view was the right one, for it is clear that there is no "right" point of view. What is clear is that, try how they will, historians see the past through the eyes of the present.

There is a final commentary on what is called historicism. Even those who are most anxious to avoid imposing their own standards on the past and strive most sincerely to see the past in its own terms are tempted to make one exception to their principle. That is in the realm of moral judgment. Let us not force the past into the straitjacket of the present, they say, but at the same time let us not suspend the eternal rules of right and wrong.

And this brings us to the troublesome problem of moral judgment in history.

Judgment in History

To judge or not to judge, that is the historical question. Should the historian sit in judgment over the great drama of the past and the men and women who performed on that vast and crowded stage, exposing evil and celebrating virtue and damning and praising famous people? Or should he or she observe the historical processes with scientific detachment, and record them as automatically as a tape recorder, rigorously excluding personal, national, or religious considerations? Is the historian competent to perform either of these functions—the function of the judge or the function of the impartial reporter?

The problem is difficult and perhaps insoluble. It raises hard questions about the purpose of history, the duties and responsibilities of the scholar, the nature of historical judgment, and the distinctions, if any, between what might be called moral and secular judgment. It raises questions, too, about the competence of any historian to judge the past and the sanctions, if any, behind such judgments as are rendered. And it requires us to weigh the dangers implicit in moral neutrality against those inherent in moral arrogance and intellectual parochialism.

Earlier generations of historians were not seriously troubled by this problem of judgment. The Greek historians, Herodotus and Thucydides, were surprisingly free from the urge to judge, but their successors in the ancient world took for granted that their function was to edify, to instruct, and to judge. Livy invited his readers to ponder the moral lessons taught by the history of Rome—as he presented it—and to observe how Rome rose to greatness through her virtues, and how the decay of these virtues brought ruin. Tacitus thought the highest function of history was to "rescue merit from oblivion," and "to hold out the reprobation of posterity as a warning and a rebuke to all base conduct." Plutarch, who wrote some sixty Moral Essays, compiled his famous *Parallel Lives* not to adorn a tale, but to point a moral, and succeeded beyond his farthest imagination.

Medieval historians knew perfectly well what were the moral standards to which history was obliged to conform, and knew, too, the penalties of nonconformity, for what was history but the working out of God's will with humankind? Even the great eighteenth-century historians, Gibbon and Hume and Robertson, Rollin and Voltaire and Raynal, accepted Bolingbroke's aphorism that history was "philosophy teaching by examples," and they assumed that its lessons were moral and that it was the duty of the historian to point them. Only with the rise of "historicism" in the nineteenth century—there were antecedents, to be sure, in such historians as Machiavelli and Vico—did the question of the propriety and the validity of moral judgment come to the fore. Ranke, and his successors and disciples in almost every country, adjured moral judgment, or said that they did, and set themselves the task of simply recording what had happened, with a minimum of comment, and with neither ostentatious approval or disapproval. Theirs was the ideal which Henry Adams later found so futile: "To satisfy himself whether, by the severest process of stating, with the least possible comment, such facts as seemed sure, in such order as seemed rigorously consequent, he could fix for a familiar moment a necessary sequence of human movement.''

There was bound to be a reaction away from this austere principle, especially as so few of its protagonists actually lived up to it. The Victorian era, which in Germany saw the triumph of historicism, was also the era of morality, of moral preaching in law and in economics, in politics and in history, as in art and in literature. It is difficult to know whether such historians as Froude in England, Michelet in France, Treitschke in Germany, or Motley in America considered themselves primarily ethical leaders or historical scholars; in fact they did not distinguish sharply between the two roles. "The external truths and rights of things," said James Anthony Froude in his inaugural address as rector of St. Andrews University, "exist independent of our thoughts or wishes, fixed as mathematics, inherent in the nature of man and the world."

To the American John L. Motley, historian of the heroic struggle of the Dutch against the Spanish rulers, and of the creation of a United Netherlands, this was the story of the struggle of Protestantism against Catholicism, of the principle of liberty against the principle of tyranny. Motley did not hesitate to pronounce moral judgment; listen to his final verdict on Philip II of Spain:

> There have been few men known to history who have been able to accomplish by their own exertions so vast an amount of evil as the king who had just died. If Philip possessed a single virtue it has eluded the conscientious research of the writer of these pages. If there are vices—as possibly there are—from which he was exempt, it is because it is not permitted to human nature to attain perfection even in evil. The only plausible explanation—for palliation there is none—of his infamous career is that the man really believed himself not a king but a God. He was placed so high above his fellow creatures as, in good faith perhaps, to believe himself incapable of doing wrong; so that whether indulging his passions or enforcing throughout the world his religious and political dogmas, he was ever conscious of embodying divine inspirations and elemental laws.[6]

And, in case his readers might think that he had stepped out of his province in thus condemning the Spanish monarch, Motley added a word on the responsibility of this historian:

> When an humble malefactor is brought before an ordinary court of justice, it is not often, in any age or country, that he escapes the pillory or the gallows because, from his own point of view, his actions, instead of being criminal, have been commendable, and because the multitude and continuity of his offenses prove him to have been sincere. And because anointed monarchs are amenable to no human tribunal, save to that terrible assize which the People, bursting its chain from time to time in the course of the ages, sets up for the trial of its oppressors, and which is called Revolution, it is more important for the great interests of humanity that before the judgment-seat of History a crown should be no protection to its wearer. There is no plea to the jurisdiction of history, if history be true to itself.
> As for the royal criminal called Philip II, his life is his arraignment, and these volumes will have been written in vain if a specification is now required.[7]

In a Carlyle or a Motley moral judgment was a form of self-indulgence. But there was more to it than this, there was high Duty! The clearest and most persuasive statement of the moral function of the historian came from Lord Acton himself. In 1895 Lord Acton was appointed Regius Professor of History at Cambridge University. In his inaugural address he exhorted his listeners, and all students of history,

> never to debase the moral currency or to lower the standards of rectitude, but to try others by the final maxim that governs your own lives, and to suffer no man and no cause to escape the undying penalty which history has the power to inflict on wrong. The plea in extenuation of guilt and mitigation of punishment is perpetual. At every step we are met by arguments which go to excuse, to palliate, to confound right and wrong and reduce the just man to the level of the reprobate...Opinions alter, manners change, creeds rise and fall, but the moral law is written on the tablets of eternity.

"We have the power," he concluded, "... to learn from undisguised and genuine records to look with remorse upon the past, and to the future with assured hope of better things; bearing this in mind, that if we lower our standard in History, we cannot uphold it in Church or State."

We cannot glibly ascribe Acton's philosophy to his Catholicism; he was, after all, not a very orthodox Catholic. Such diverse contemporary historians as Veronica Wedgwood, Isaiah Berlin, and Arnold Toynbee—none of them Catholic—all come out for the obligation, or the necessity, of moral judgment in history. Thus Wedgwood, who has done so much to illuminate the great political and religious issues that stirred England in the seventeenth century, warns us against

> the confusion into which historians fall when they make allowances for "the standards of the age." Their intention is to understand and be just to the past, but the result in the long run may be unfair to the present, because this outlook steadily and stealthily fosters the conviction that nothing is good or bad in itself, but only in relation to its surroundings... the aspiration to understand and to forgive is noble and valid in personal relationships between the living but [she concludes] the application of the principle of...forgiveness to historical personages is a sentimental fallacy. [8]

Arnold Toynbee, who has concerned himself more consistently with the universal and the eternal than any other modern historian, has remained throughout his distinguished career a Christian moralist, ready to judge the quick and the dead; his assertion that the expulsion of the Arabs from Palestine by the Israelis was no less a crime than the Nazi murder of some six million Jews precipitated an international controversy.

All of this constitutes what might be called a moral argument in favor of moral judgment. The moral laws are universal and timeless; murder is always murder and betrayal is always betrayal, cruelty and intolerance are always the same, the historian cannot stand above the moral laws, or stand aside from them, but must acknowledge them and participate in them and apply them. If the historian does not, he or she will fail the cause of morality—and of history as well—and forfeit the confidence and respect of peers.

There is, however, another and perhaps more persuasive argument for moral judgment in history, one that rests not so much on moral as on psychological grounds. It is this: that the historian cannot, in any event, help himself, and that he might as well acknowledge what is inherent and implicit in his condition. He is, after all, a creature of his time, his society, his faith. Even if he resolutely refrains from overt moral judgment, he will surely be guilty of covert judgment: his choice of subject, his selection of facts, his very vocabulary will betray him. How much better, then, how much fairer and more honest, to acknowledge his position in advance; how much better to call his book—it is Charles A. Beard who makes the point—*An Economic Interpretation of the Constitution* rather than to fall back on a title like *The Making of the Constitution,* one which "does not advise the reader at the outset concerning the upshot to be expected." History is not a science, and the historian is not a scientist. "The supreme command," therefore, "is that he must cast off his servitude to the assumptions of natural science and return to his own subject matter—to history as actuality."

This is the argument, too, of the distinguished Oxford philosopher, Sir Isaiah Berlin, who sees in the passion for scientific impartiality yet another expression of the misguided and pernicious belief that history is a science. "The case against the notion of historical objectivity," he writes, "is like the case against international law, or international morality; that it does not exist." And he adds the warning that

> except on the assumption that history must deal with human beings purely as material objects in space, must in short, be behaviourist—its method can scarcely be assimilated to the standards of an exact natural science. The invocation to historians to suppress even that minimal degree of moral or psychological evaluation which is necessarily involved in viewing human beings as creatures with purposes and motives…seems to me to rest upon a confusion of the aims and methods of the humane studies with those of natural science. It is one of the greatest and most destructive fallacies of the last hundred years. [9]

But the stout champions of moral judgment do not have things all their own way. Not at all. Here comes a whole phalanx of historians with a formidable arsenal of counter-arguments.

First, while it is true that history tries to observe something like historical "due process," it cannot in the nature of the case do so. The past is not there to defend itself. We cannot recall the witnesses, put them on the stand, question and cross-examine them. It is difficult enough to render a moral verdict on anything so recent as, let us say, Hoover's dispersion of the "bonus army," or the conduct of the Vichy government, or the resort to the atomic weapon at Hiroshima; how much more difficult, then, to sit in judgment on the character of Alcibiades, the justification for the murder of Caesar, the conduct of the Norman invaders of England, or of the Spanish conquistadores.

Second, while technical judgment is essential, in the law, in the civil service, in the university, in athletics, if society is to function, such judgment does not pretend to be moral but professional. A university professor who permitted his moral views of a candidate to dictate his grades, a referee whose decisions were based on moral considerations, even a judge who allowed private moral convictions to influence decisions on questions of contracts, wills, liability, or bankruptcy proceedings, would be regarded as not only incompetent but expendable. There are reasonably clear standards for such practical judgments as society requires—laws, rules, tests—but as parents, psychiatrists, and priests so well know, moral judgments present questions of labyrinthine complexity even when all the relevant evidence appears to be available. Where history is concerned, the conduct of people or of nations in past centuries, all the relevant evidence is never available, and there are no universal standards. What the historian does, when he or she judges, is merely to identify his or her own "can't-help-but-believe" with eternal verities. Herodotus made this point twenty-five centuries ago: When Darius was upon the throne, he summoned

> into his presence the Hellenes at his court and asked them for what price they would consent to make a meal of their fathers when they died. The Hellenes replied that all the money in the World would not induce them to do such a thing, whereupon Darius summoned the Callatian Indians, who do eat their parents, and asked them (in the presence of the Hellenes, who were kept informed, through an interpreter, of the tenour of the conversation) for what price they would be willing to burn their fathers when they died. The Indians shrieked aloud and begged him not to pursue an unmentionable subject—a story which illustrates the habitual attitude of Mankind towards this question, and which, in my opinion, justifies Pindar's poetic aphorism that "Custom is king of all." [10]

Justice Holmes made the point with even greater succinctness. "I prefer champagne to ditch-water," he said, "but I see no reason to suppose the cosmos does."

If history "tells us" anything, it tells us that standards, values, and principles have varied greatly from age to age and from society to society; indeed, that they have varied greatly from one generation to another within the same society. Popes chosen for their learning and their virtue were certain that morality required that they put down heresies with fire and sword, cruelty and torture; sixteenth-century Europeans had no compunction about killing Indians because the Indians had no souls; learned and upright Puritans readily sent witches to their death; and nineteenth-century Christians in the American South regarded slavery as a blessing. The Hellenes of whom Herodotus tells us were no more shocked at the notion of eating their dead fathers than we are at Hellenic notions of love. Consider, for example, Plato's defense of a practice which most of our contemporaries regard not only as immoral but as pernicious, and which our military and civil authorities combat with sleepless zeal:

> I cannot say what greater benefit can fall to the lot of a young man than a virtuous lover and to the lover than a beloved youth... If then there were any means whereby a state or army could be formed of lovers and favorites, they would administer affairs better than all others, provided they abstain from all disgraceful deeds and compete with one another in honest rivalry, and such men, together with others like them, though few in number, so to speak would conquer the world. [11]

A problem which has confronted, and perplexed, American historians for a hundred years is slavery. Surely if anything is wrong, slavery is wrong. No social institution more deeply offends our moral sensibilities than this; no other collective experience induces in us a comparable sense of shame. Slavery, we are all agreed, corrupts alike the slave and the master; slavery corrupts the body politic, the poison still infects us.

This is the vocabulary of morality, and it is this vocabulary which we invoke, almost instinctively, when ever we discuss what was long euphemistically called the "peculiar institution."

Yet when we come to pronounce judgment on slavery we are met, at the very threshold, with the most intransigent consideration—that generation after generation of good, humane, Christian men and women not only accepted it, but considered it a blessing. What are we to say when confronted by the fact—a formidable body of evidence permits us to use that word—that our own forebears, only two or three generations back, embraced slavery, rejoiced in it, fought to defend it, and gave up their lives confident that they were dying in a good cause.

Clearly, we cannot fall back on the simple explanation that all these men and women—those who owned slaves and those who sustained the slave system— were bad. These beneficiaries of and defenders of slavery were neither better nor worse than their cousins north of the Mason and Dixon line who had managed to get rid of the "peculiar institution" one or two generations earlier; they were neither better nor worse than we are. Whatever may be said, on practical grounds, for the moral righteousness and self-righteousness of abolitionists who fought slavery, it can be said that no comparable pressures weigh upon us as historians. It is absurd for us to pass moral judgment on slave-holders, absurd to indict a whole people or to banish a whole people to some historical purgatory where they can expiate their sins. Lincoln saw this, Lincoln who saw so much. The people of the North and the South, he said in his second inaugural address, "read the same Bible and pray to the same God, and each invokes His aid against the other. It may seem strange that any men should dare to ask a just God's assistance in wringing their bread from the sweat of other men's faces. But let us judge not, that we be not judged."

We can agree now, most of us, that slavery was an unmitigated evil, but we cannot therefrom conclude that those who inherited it, were caught in it and by it, supported it and fought for it, were evil people. What we can say is that but for the grace of God, or the accident of history, we might ourselves have been caught up in slavery, and bound by it, and habituated to accepting it, just as our forebears were. What we can says is that if earlier generations—North and South alike—bore the burden and the guilt of slavery, we have borne the burden, and the guilt, of racial discrimination, and that morally there is not much to choose between the two.

Clearly, different generations have different moral standards; it is a form of intellectual arrogance for us to impose ours upon the past. We do not accept ex post facto laws, bills of attainder, or guilt by association in our legal system; we should not apply these concepts or rules retroactively to the past. Far better to refrain from the folly and the vanity of moral righteousness about the past; far better to accept Lincoln's admonition to judge not, that we be not judged. The historian's task is not to judge, but to understand. How did it happen that people dedicated to carrying out the precepts of the Sermon on the Mount could send those who disagreed with them to the stake? How did it happen that people dedicated to the expansion of European civilization could carry fire and sword to the hapless inhabitants of the American continents? How did it happen that men and women who dearly loved their own children and whose daily lives were bound each to each with natural piety could bitterly oppose laws designed to protect little children from the awful burden of work in factory and mine? How did it happen that Christian men and women could look upon slavery as a blessing? How did it happen that a people who boasted a high civilization, who had produced Leibniz and Kant, Beethoven and Mozart, Goethe and Heine, Rilke and Thomas Mann, could stand by while six million Jews were done to death?

Tout comprendre, tout pardonner. But it does not follow that the historian who understands all forgives all. It is the historian's business to "understand"; it is not the historian's business either to condemn or to forgive. The historian is not God.

For here is a third argument against moral judgment in history—that the historian is not God. He is not called upon to judge the quick or the dead; indeed he is not called upon to judge. If he sets up as a judge he changes the whole pattern of his intellectual and professional role from one dedicated to objective inquiry to one devoted to prosecution or defense. As the distinguished historian of the Russian Revolution, E. J. Carr, observes, the attempt to erect standards of historical judgment "is itself unhistorical and contradicts the very essence of history. It provides a dogmatic answer to questions which the historian is bound, by his vocation, incessantly to ask. The historian who accepts answers in advance to these questions, goes to work with his eyes blindfolded, and, renounces his vocation."

The historian is not God; he or she is a person and like other people. The historian confesses most of the failings, responds to most of the pressures, succumbs to most of the temptations that afflict his or her fellow human beings. Consciously or unconsciously, the historian is almost always taking sides. Can we really trust Carlyle on Cromwell or Motley on Philip II or Charles A. Beard on the causes of the Civil War or Vernon Parrington on John Marshall? Can we trust either Macaulay or Winston Churchill to write impartially about the Duke of Marlborough? Can we trust Lord Acton or Benedetto Croce on a subject so close to their hearts as the history of liberty? Clearly we cannot. The historian, like the judge, the priest, or the statesman, is a creature of his or her race, nationality, religion, class, inheritance, and education, and can never emancipate himself or herself from these formative influences and achieve Olympian impartiality. Where the historian undertakes to *judge* he or she does not even have the prop of professional training and traditions to sustain him or her as he or she does when recording and reconstructing. The historian's judgments are, therefore, as Herbert Butterfield has observed, but "pseudo-moral judgments, masquerading as moral ones, mixed and muddy affairs, part prejudice, part political animosity, with a dash of ethical flavoring wildly tossed into the concoction." And because not even a Ranke, not even a Mommsen, not even a Toynbee, can survey the whole of history, his forays into the past are bound to be haphazard and fortuitous as well. For purposes of reconstructing the past, that is not a fatal handicap; others will fill in the gaps. But for purposes of formulating a moral code and applying it systematically and impartially, it is a fatal handicap.

We may, then, accept the findings of the historian in matters of fact—always subject to subsequent revision, to be sure—but why should we accept his conclusions in matters of morality? "I beseech you in the bowels of Christ," wrote Oliver Cromwell in his Letter to the Church of Scotland, "think it possible you may be mistaken." Alas, the historians have so often been mistaken. Over the centuries they have stood ready to pronounce judgments which differ little from the tainted and tarnished judgments of statesmen, soldiers, and priests. Catholic historians have sustained the persecution of Protestant heretics, and Protestant historians looked with equanimity upon the persecution of Catholics. National historians have almost invariably defended and justified the conduct of their own nation and as regularly rendered judgment against the enemies of their nation; more, they have themselves provided the arguments for chauvinistic nationalism, imperialism; and militarism. No wonder that the chief professional preoccupation of the historian in our day is revision!

There is no special dispensation for historians. They are not exempt from the prejudices, the ambitions, the vanities, the fears that afflict their fellow human beings. When they don their professional robes they are impressive and sometimes majestic figures; when they are persuaded to put on the robes of the moral judge, they are often as naked as the unhappy emperor of Hans Andersen's story.

We come then to a fourth consideration, practical rather than philosophical: the futility of moral judgment in history. Surely, say those who insist that the historian be a judge, it is proper that the historian reprobate the Inquisition and exalt tolerance, that he deplore slavery and celebrate freedom, that he execrate Hitler and Nazi genocide and rejoice in the triumph of the forces of liberation. But why should the historian go out of his way to condemn or to praise these things? The assumption behind this expectation is that readers have no mind of their own, no moral standards, no capacity to exercise judgment; that they are incapable of distinguishing between slavery and freedom, persecution and tolerance, but depend upon the historian to do this for them. Are those mature enough to read serious histories really so obtuse that they cannot draw conclusions from the facts that are submitted to them? Is there really any danger that students will yearn for slavery or rejoice in the Inquisition or admire Philip II or Adolf Hitler if the historian does not bustle in and set them right? Alas, if readers do not know that Hitler was a moral monster and that the murder of six million Jews was a moral outrage, nothing the historian can say will set them right; if they do not know in their bones that slavery corrupts both slave and master, nothing the historian can say will enlighten them. Is there not, indeed, some danger that if the historian continually usurps the role of judge, readers may react against his judgments; that if the historian insists on treating his readers as morally incompetent, they may turn away from history altogether to some more mature form of literature?

There is a further consideration, which might be called a plea in abatement. It is this: that the problem of judgment may be trusted to take care of itself. No reader comes wholly unprepared to the contemplation of a chapter of history; he brings with him his own education, his own moral and philosophical outlook. Nor is the student ever confined to a single account of any important chapter of history. We can be confident that historians will differ in their interpretation of the past and that these differences will be available and familiar to readers. Errors will be corrected; wrong opinions will be set right. For every historian who defends Bristish policy in Ireland there will be one to expose it and reprobate it; for every historian who paints slavery in sunlight terms, there will be one to expose its darkness and cruelty; for every historian who places responsibility for the First World War squarely at the door of the Germans, there will be one ready to make clear that it was the Russians or the French who were really to blame. Let the historian learn humility: the reader is not dependent upon the historian for the whole of his or her history; he or she is not dependent upon the historian for moral instruction.

That is what the great Italian historical philosopher Benedetto Croce meant when he wrote that "those who, on the plea of narrating history, bustle about as judges, condemning here and giving absolution there, because they think that this is the office of history, are generally recognized as devoid of historical sense."

One final observation is appropriate. We should not confuse moral with professional judgment. In the field of his professional competence the scholar has the same obligation as the judge, the teacher, the physician, the architect. The judge who pronounces sentence, the teacher who gives a grade, the physician who diagnoses an illness, the architect who condemns a building is not indulging in moral but exercising professional judgment. So the historian who, after painstaking study of all available evidence, and after cleansing himself of all the perilous stuff which might distort his vision, concludes that Lee did right to surrender at Appomattox rather than fight it out in the west, that Roosevelt was not responsible for the attack on Pearl Harbor, that the conduct of the Crimean War was characterized by criminal folly, that the violation of Belgian neutrality in 1914 was an error of the first magnitude, that Cavour rather than Garibaldi deserves credit for Italian unification, that Shakespeare and not Bacon wrote *Hamlet,* that only the stone and not the inscription on the Kensington rune stone is genuine, and that the Protocols of Zion are forgeries, is performing his professional duty. The historian may be mistaken—but so may the judge, the teacher, the physician—that is a chance society takes. His or her judgments may have moral overtones—it is difficult to keep those out, and we have learned to discount them, But if it is exasperating to find a Carlyle or a Motley laying down the moral laws for us, it is equally exasperating to discover that when you lay all the scholarly investigators of a subject end to end, they do not reach a conclusion.

Notes

1. Henry Adams, *The Education of Henry Adams* (Boston: Houghton Mifflin Co., 1918), p. 382.
2. Charles A. Beard, *The Open Door at Home* (New York: The Macmillan Co.), p. 14.
3. Henry Steele Commager, *Theodore Parker* (Boston: Little, Brown and Co., 1936), preface.
4. Paul Hazard, *European Thought in the Eighteenth Century* (London: Hollis and Carter, 1954), pp. 249–500.
5. Adams, *The Education of Henry Adams,* p. 382.
6. John L. Motley, *United Netherlands,* vol. 5 (New York, 1868), pp. 74–75.
7. Ibid., p. 79.
8. Veronica Wedgwood, *Truth and Opinion* (New York: The Macmillan Co.,1965), pp. 48–49.
9. Sir Isaiah Berlin, *Historical Inevitability* (Oxford: Oxford University Press, 1954), pp. 52–53.
10. Herodotus.
11. Plato, *Symposium,* p. 178.

five

History as Law and as Philosophy

The Use of History

We are all acquainted with the young man who earnestly assures us, with a mixture of vanity and zeal, that he has always "hated history." It is all dates, he tells us, or it is all a lot of rather tiresome problems—the problem of the "fall" of Rome, the problem of the French Revolution, the problem of secession and Civil War. And it never gets you anywhere; you are no better off when you have finished than when you began.

Some of this attitude may be confidently set down to poor and uninspiring teaching—teaching which never challenged the interest nor excited the imagination of students. Some of it—perhaps a good deal—may be put down to the same kind of uninspired teaching embodied in textbooks in which the authors try to please everybody, avoid the "controversial," ignore the dramatic, concentrate on problems which are never solved or whose solution is of no interest, and, like so many of the novels and dramas of our time, eschew narrative and leave out heroes and villains. Some of it can be ascribed to the individual himself; his inability to respond imaginatively to the drama of the past.

But after we have done all this explaining, there remains a stubborn residuum of intelligent and open-minded students who still find nothing to nourish them in history. They may agree with Gibbon that history is "the register of the follies and misfortunes of mankind," or with Napoleon that it is a "lie agreed upon," or with Carlyle that it is "a great dust-heap," and they do not stop to read those marvelous volumes in which Gibbon recorded the "follies and misfortunes" of man, or discover how Carlyle proved that history was charged with life and passion, nor are they excited by the challenge to separate truth from lies about Napoleon himself.

What are we to say to all this? Why should the young study history? Why should their elders read history, or write it?

That is a question which recurs again and again: What use is history? Let us admit at once that in a practical way history has no use, let us concede that it is not good for anything that can be weighed, measured, or counted. It will not solve problems; it will not guarantee us against the errors of the past; it will not show nations how to avoid wars, or how to win them; it will not provide scientific explanations of depressions or keys to prosperity; it will not contribute in any overt way to progress.

But the same can be said, of course, of many other things which society values and which people cherish. What use, after all, is a Mozart sonata or a painting by Renoir, or a statue by Milles? What use is the cathedral of Siena or the rose windows of Chartres or a novel by Flaubert or a sonnet by Wordsworth? What use, for that matter, are a great many mundane things which society takes for granted and on which it lavishes thought and effort: a baseball game, for example, or a rose garden, or a brocade dress, or a bottle of port?

Happily, a civilized society does not devote all of its thought and effort to things whose usefulness can be statistically demonstrated. There are other criteria than that of usefulness, and other meanings to the term *useful* than those acknowledged by the Thomas Gradgrinds of this world.

History, we can confidently assert, is useful in the sense that art and music, poetry and flowers, religion and philosophy are useful. Without it—as without these—life would be poorer and meaner; without it we should be denied some of those intellectual and moral experiences which give meaning and richness to life. Surely it is no accident that the study of history has been the solace of many of the noblest minds of every generation.

The first and doubtless the richest pleasure of history is that it adds new dimensions to life itself, enormously extending our perspective and enlarging our experience. It permits us to enter vicariously into the past, to project our vision back over thousands of years and enlarge it to embrace all races of humankind. Through the pages of history we can hear Pericles deliver his funeral oration, trek with the Crusaders to the Holy Land, sail with Columbus past the gates of Hercules and to a new world, share the life of Goethe and Schiller at the little court of Weimar, stand and listen to those stirring debates in those dusty prairie towns which sent Douglas to the Senate and Lincoln to the White House, stand beside Winston Churchill as he rallies the people of Britain to their finest hour. History supplies to us all those elements which Henry James thought essential to the life of the mind: density, variety, intricacy, richness, in the pattern of thought and of action, and with it "the sense of the past."

This immense enlargement of experience means, of course, that history provides us with great companions on our journey through life. This is so familiar a consideration that it needs no elaboration. Wherever the historian or biographer has been, he or she has given new depth and range to our associations. We have but to take down the books and we are admitted to the confidence of Voltaire and Rousseau, Johnson and Boswell, Thomas Jefferson and John Adams, Justice Holmes and William James. We can know them with more of an intimacy than their contemporaries knew them, for we can read their letters, journals and diaries. This is not just one of the pleasures of history, it is one of the indispensable pleasures of life.

A third, and familiar, pleasure of history is the experience of identifying the present with the past, and thus adding a new dimension to places and events. It was Macaulay who observed that "the pleasure of History is analogous in many respects to that produced by foreign travel. The student is transported into a new state of society. He sees new fashions. He hears new modes of expression. His mind is enlarged by contemplating the wide diversities of laws, of morals, and of manners." George Macaulay Trevelyan—himself a grand-nephew of Macaulay—has conjured up this pleasure for us in one of his most glowing passages:

> Places, like books, have an interest or a beauty of association, as well as an absolute or aesthetic beauty. The garden front of St. John's, Oxford, is beautiful to everyone; but for the lover of history its outward charm is blent with the intimate feelings of his own mind, with images of that same college as it was during the Great Civil War. Given over to the use of a Court whose days of royalty were numbered, its walks and quadrangles were filled, as the end came near, with men and women learning to accept sorrow as their lot through life, the ambitious abandoning hope of power, the wealthy hardening themselves to embrace poverty, those who loved England preparing to sail for foreign shores, and lovers to be parted forever. There they strolled through the garden, as the hopeless evenings fell, listening, at the end of all, while the siege guns broke the silence with ominous iteration. Behind the cannon on those low hills to northward were ranked the inexorable men who came to lay their hands on all this beauty, hoping to change it to strength and sterner virtue.[1]

Everyone who has visited historic towns, in the Old World or the New, knows that when he or she looks at them through the eyes of history they cease to be museum pieces and pulse with life and with vigor. Nestling between its ancient hills, bisected by the gleaming Arno, its domes and towers piercing the skies, Florence is beautiful to the eyes of even the purblind. But how it springs into life when we people its piazzas and narrow streets with the men and women of the past: when we conjure up the spectacle of Savonarola burned at the stake in the great Piazza de la Signoria where the mighty David now stands; Brunelleschi erecting the giant Duomo; Ghiberti carving the great bronze doors of the Baptistry; Raphael and Leonardo and Michelangelo painting those pictures which now hang in such lavish profusion from the glittering walls of the Uffizi and the Pitti palaces; Machiavelli pondering the history of the condottieri; and Galileo seeing a new universe through his telescope and opening up a new universe of the mind as well. Did ever a city boast a comparable galaxy of genius; did ever a city publish itself more generously in its monuments, or impress itself more richly on the eye and on the mind?

Nor is it only the great centers of art and letters, like Florence or Venice or Salzburg, that take on new dimensions when seen through the eyes of history; the same miracle transforms even the most modest of towns. Henry James observed, somewhat condescendingly, that Emerson had "dwelt for fifty years within the undecorated walls of his youth"; but to Emerson those rooms were redolent of the past, as was the little village of Concord. And as for Hawthorne, how, wrote James, could he have found materials for his stories, living where he did, where "the coldness, the thinness, the blankness... present themselves so vividly that our foremost feeling is that of compassion for a romancer looking for subjects in such a field." But Hawthorne himself looked out of his attic window on a Salem rich in history and tradition and found in it the ingredients for *The Scarlet Letter* and *The House of the Seven Gables,* and a dozen other stories that are a precious part of our literature.

Consider the little town of Salem in Massachusetts, now no more than a suburb of Boston. It is a lovely town in its own right, there by the sea and the rocks, its handsome old houses still standing sedately along Chestnut and Federal streets. As we look at it through the eyes of history we conjure up a straggling village busy with fishing and with theological disputes and remember that Roger Williams preached here those heresies which brought him banishment from the Bay Colony, and so too Anne Hutchinson. We look at Gallows Hill and recall the dark and terrifying story of Salem witchcraft. We recreate it in its heyday, when its captains sailed all the waters of the globe and the spoils and rewards of the China trade glittered in every drawing room. For at the turn of the century Salem was like one of the famous city-states of Italy—Florence or Venice or Pisa. It had its own architects, like Samuel McIntyre who built the stately mansions of the sea captains and the merchant princes; its own preachers, like the famous William Bentley of the East Church, reputed to be the most learned man in America; its own jurists, like Samuel Putnam and Samuel Sewall who became Chief Justices of the Commonwealth, and Joseph Story who joined the Supreme Court of the United States at thirty-two. Samuel Bowditch was a boy here, learning celestial mathematics and navigation, sailing on a Salem merchantman, and growing up to write the *Practical Navigator.* So was George Crowninshield who built the magnificent Cleopatra's Barge and sailed it through the Mediterranean, and the dour Timothy Pickering who lived in the oldest house in town and grew up to be the most reactionary politician in the country; so too the astonishing Benjamin Thompson who grew up to be Count Rumford of the Holy Roman Empire and found the Royal Institution in London; and so too William Prescott who became the historian of Mexico and of Peru. —Then another generation, and Salem entered its long decline, its harbors silted up and its wharfs fell into decay and grass grew up between the cobblestones of its ancient streets, while the paint peeled off the proud McIntyre houses. It is all there—in Nathaniel Hawthorne's stories, in the reminiscences of Joseph Story and Rufus Choate, in the historical romances by Joseph Hergesheimer and Esther Forbes, so faithful to the spirit and the reality of the old town—all there for us to recapture through the pages of history.

Needless to say, all this makes great demands upon the imagination, the imagination of the historian and of the student alike. "At bottom," George Macaulay Trevelyan has said, "the appeal of history is imaginative," and he gives us, as an example of this, one of Carlyle's recreations of the past—it is in his essay on Boswell's Johnson:

> Rough Samuel and sleek wheedling James *were,* and *are not.* Their Life and whole personal Environment has melted into air. The Mitre Tavern still stands in Fleet Street; but where now is its scot-and-lot paying, beef-and-ale loving, cocked-hatted, pot-bellied Landlord; its rosy-faced assiduous Landlady, with all her shining brass-pans, waxed tables, well-filled larder-shelves; her cooks and bootjacks, and errand boys and watery-mouthed hangers-on? Gone! Gone! The becking Waiter, who, with wreathed smiles, was wont to spread for Samuel and Bozzy their supper of the gods, has long since pocketed his last sixpence; and vanished, sixpences and all, like a ghost at cock-crowing.

> The Bottles they drank out of are all broken, the Chairs they sat on all rotted and burnt; the very Knives and Forks they ate with have rusted to the heart, and become brown oxide of iron, and mingled with the indiscriminate clay. All, all has vanished; in very deed and truth, like that baseless fabric of Prospero's air-vision. Of the Mitre Tavern nothing but the bare walls remain there; of London, of England, of the World, nothing but the bare walls remain; and these also decaying (were they of adamant), only slower. [2]

A dangerous thing, this, for once we introduce the element of imagination we imperil the integrity of the historical record. Yet how can we possibly exclude it? What is history, after all, without imagination? Imagination comes to our aid at every moment; it is what permits us to clothe the bare bones of history with life. It throws a glow over the most impersonal, the dullest, of the data of history. It infuses even a statistical table with color and life: who can read the statistics of the population growth of the western territories and states of the United States in the nineteenth century without seeing, in his mind's eye, the Conestoga wagon, and the canal boats on the Erie Canal, the railroad puffing its way across the Appalachians, weather-beaten men with their wives and children and cattle, beating out a trail to Oregon or to the Mormon utopia at the Great Salt Lake?

Imagination brings home to us that the names in the history books represent real people, that the decisions which were made involved the same fears and hopes and uncertainties and courage as those which we ourselves make, that Latimer at the stake and Lord Nelson at Trafalgar suffered the same agonies and exaltations which we ourselves experience, that to a man like Robert E. Lee the decision to stay with his state was no abstract "problem" of secession, but just such a spiritual and moral crisis as would plunge us into despair if we confronted it today. Alas, many historians are like the preacher of whom Emerson writes:

> A snow-storm was falling around us. The snow-storm was real, the preacher merely spectral, and the eye felt the sad contrast in looking at him, and then, out of the window behind him into the beautiful meteor of the snow. He had lived in vain. He had no one word intimating that he had laughed or wept, was married or in love, had been commended, or cheated, or chagrined. If he had ever lived and acted, we were none the wiser for it. The capital secret of his profession, namely to convert life into truth, he had not learned . . . This man had ploughed and planted and talked and bought and sold; he had read books; he had eaten and drunken; his head aches, his heart throbs; he smiles and suffers; yet was there not a surmise, a hint, in all the discourse, that he had ever lived at all. [3]

It might be thought that imagination like—let us say—an ear for music, is something you either have or have not. If you have it, well and good; if not, there is nothing to be done about it. But the imagination, like a taste for music, or for painting, can be cultivated. How can the historical imagination be cultivated? It can be cultivated through drama and poetry. Shakespeare suffused the stuff of history with his glorious imagination; no wonder Winston Churchill said that he had learned all of his English history out of Shakespeare! How history comes alive in the novels of Walter Scott—such varied historians as Prescott and Carlyle and Trevelyan have acknowledged his inspiration. With what insight does Wordsworth read its moral lessons, in the sonnet "On the Extinction of the Venetian Republic," for example, or in "To Toussaint L'Ouverture," or in *The Prelude*. Imagination can be cultivated, too, by the study of art and architecture. Who can wander through the National Portrait Gallery in London and not feel stirred by the spectacle of these men and women who have made England; how exhilarating to visit such great Palladian palaces as the Villa Rotonda and the Villa Malcontenta outside Vicenza, and to see Jefferson's Monticello emerge out of these models.

This does not exhaust the pleasures of history; they are, indeed, inexhaustible. We may, without too gross an impropriety, paraphrase Dr. Johnson's observations on London, that anyone who is tired of history is tired of life.

Can we go beyond the pleasures of history to laws of history, or even to the philosophy of history? That all depends on what you mean by *laws* and by *philosophy*.

Causation in History

One of the liveliest pleasures of history is that, more continuously and more persuasively than almost any other study, it nourishes and enlists the reflective faculties. Nowhere are those faculties more busily engaged than in seeking for causes.

"Happy is he who knows the causes of things." But if this is true then it can be said that historians are forever pursuing happiness, but never quite attaining it. The search for the causes of things is, and has long been, the chief preoccupation of thoughtful historians. No self-respecting modern historian is content merely with recording what happened; he or she wants to explain why it happened. Of all problems of history, causation is the most urgent, the most fascinating, and the most baffling.

Why did history turn out the way it did? Why were the Chinese ahead of the West in civilization? Why did civilization flourish so spectacularly in Greece at a time when most of Europe was lost in what we think of as barbarism? Why were Europeans so far in advance of Americans for so many centuries? Why did the Roman Empire "decline and fall"? Why were the Moslems able to conquer so much of Europe and why did Moslem power ebb? What explains the amazing vitality of the Vikings and then of the Norsemen who swarmed over seas and over land, and carried their culture to the shores of Ireland and France and Sicily, and then fell back into obscurity? How did it happen that a little fog-bound island off the north coast of Europe came to be one of the greatest world powers, and that the English language—of all unlikely languages—came to be spoken from London to Singapore and from Toronto to the Cape of Good Hope? Why did the American colonies break away from the Mother Country, and why were they successful in their revolution? Why did the southern states break away from the American Union and why was their revolution unsuccessful? Why did British America become two great countries, while Latin America fragmented into more than twenty? Why do only English-speaking peoples have a two-party system while all others have a one-or a multiparty system? What caused the two great wars of the twentieth century? What explains the spread and the triumphs of Communism? How can one explain the change in styles, from classical to romantic, from romantic to modern? How can one explain the change in moral standards from age to age—the changing attitude toward slavery, for example, or toward child labor or toward sex?

For over two thousand years philosophers and historians have tried to answer these and similar questions about the course of history, though it is only in the last two or three centuries that the inquiry has been both open-minded and independent. Socrates, in one of the most famous of his discourses, asserted the validity of inquiry: "That we shall be better and braver and less helpless if we think that we ought to enquire than we should have been if we indulged in the idle fancy that there was no knowing and no use in seeking to know what we do not know—that is a theme upon which I am ready to fight in word and deed to the utmost of my power."

Yet most ancient historians did, in fact, indulge in something very like "idle fancy." The great Greek and Roman historians rarely inquired into the causes of things; it was enough for them that whatever happened was bound to happen, that it was all in the hands of the gods or of fate. Even so great a historian as Thucydides does not seek the deeper causes of the Peloponnesian War or the defeat of Athens, nor does a moralist like Plutarch inquire into the explanation for the virtues and the vices which he describes.

Christian historians, too, had an easy time of it. Everything that happened in history, from the sparrow that fell to the earth to the fall of empires, had a cause: it was all the working out of a divine plan. St. Augustine had made this clear, once and for all, in *The City of God,* and thereafter it was accepted without serious question. It is hard for us to realize, now, how this simplistic theory dominated historical thinking for more than a thousand years, how it persisted, even, well past the Renaissance and Reformation and down to the Age of Reason. Thus it was in the seventeenth century that the great French historian Jacques Bossuet prepared his *Discourses on Universal History* to demonstrate that the whole course of history was but the working out of a divine plan which happened, also, to be the plan of the Catholic popes. And at almost the same time, Bossuet's American contemporary, Edward Johnson, explained the planting of the Bay Colony under the title *The Wonder-Working Providence of Sion's Saviour in New England.* Or consider the great debate over the meaning and the explanation of America which raged from the fifteenth to the eighteenth centuries. How could one explain the New World? How could one explain its primitive state, the backwardness of its native races, the absence of organized society, or government? Every historian and philosopher who addressed himself to this problem started with the Flood, postulating for the New World a later Flood or a greater Flood or a series of Floods; all, too, with few exceptions, took for granted that humankind in every continent was descended from a common set of ancestors, Adam and Eve.

The mental habit of ascribing historical events, great and small, to the caprice of the gods or to the inscrutable will of God, persisted even into the eighteenth century: thus the popularity of cyclical theories of history or of what might be called the "ebb and flow" theory, as illustrated by *The Grandeur and Decadence of Rome,* or the *Decline and Fall of the Roman Empire, Westward the Star of Empire,* and other books with titles of a like nature. So, too, did the habit of acknowledging the authority of impersonal law, only now it was secular, not divine law, now it was "the law of Nature" as well as of "Nature's God." This was the Newtonian theory applied to the affairs of men, and it had the immense advantage of making history not only a secular but a rational affair. Soon all the historians and philosophers were explaining history in terms of nature, and in one way or another this has persisted down to our own time. The eighteenth-century concept of nature and nature's law was, however, very different from ours: nature was orderly, rational, and, in a curious way, anthropocentric. The universe, as humans knew it, was ruled by law that operated harmoniously and implacably, like some great mechanism; as people were part of the universe, they, too, were subject to universal law. Oddly enough this did not turn out to be deterministic in any malign sense. For the laws which controlled the universe were harmonious and rational. That meant that they applied to society and government as well as to the courses of the stars or the ebb and flow of the tides, and it meant that they could be apprehended and adopted by the reason of human-kind. If people could but conform to these laws of nature instead of ignoring them or flouting them, the miseries and agonies that had so long afflicted them would disappear, and peace, prosperity, and progress would usher in a millenium.

Curiously enough, though the faith in reason evaporated, reliance on force persisted in a more sophisticated form down to our own time. Montesquieu had argued the importance of "climate" in history—a term which he used much as we would use the term *environment*, and since his day climate or geography has been one of the most popular of all explanations of history. The Abbé Raynal used it to explain the backwardness of the Americas; and after him a host of scholars and scientists as diverse as Alexander von Humboldt and Henry T. Buckle, Richard Green and Friedrich Raetzel, Frederick Jackson Turner and Brooks Adams cele-brated the predominant role of climate and geography in guiding the destinies of man. But climate and geography were by no means the only impersonal forces which won the allegiance of historians. Karl Marx founded a school of history, and not of history alone, which interpreted most of the activities and ideas of people in terms of economic interests and forces. Admiral Mahan worshipped sea power as a kind of brooding omniscience in history; Henry Adams insisted quite simply on force—first—and for many centuries—the force of religion, then, in modern times, coal, steam, and electricity as symbolized in the dynamo. "The historians' business," wrote Henry Adams, "was to follow the track of energy" wherever it led, and that is what he did, until he came at last to radium and to atomic power. "Power leaped from every atom, and enough of it to supply the stellar universe showed itself running to waste at every pore of matter. Man could no longer hold it off. Forces grasped his wrist and flung him about as though he had hold of a live wire."[4]

The "forces of the stellar universe" were impersonal and aimless; if history was indeed controlled by such forces, there was no possibility of reducing it to law—just what Adams concluded when he somewhat perversely hit upon the law of the dissipation of energy as the sovereign law of history. But the eighteenth century had invented and the nineteenth had perfected a new and more benign force. Progress was the new idea and the new force; progress first within the framework of natural law and then within the framework of evolution. Turgot had announced it in a memorable address in 1750; the Encyclopaedists had embraced it, and with Con-dorcet it became well-nigh official.

The doctrine of progress was confirmed by faith rather than by observation, and sometimes—as Voltaire made clear in *Candide* or Dr. Johnson in *Rasselas*—faith gave way to skepticism. It lacked historical support—had there really been progress in the oldest societies such as China or Egypt or Greece?—and it lacked scientific support, as well. How fortunate, then, that the doctrine of evolution appeared to provide it with the strongest scientific support, at least the doctrine of evolution according to Herbert Spencer. For Spencer made clear that the great, transcendent laws of organic evolution which regulated the animal world, regulated the world of human beings as well. As evolution assured the survival of the fittest in the world of nature, so it guaranteed that humans, too, would progress toward perfection by the elimination of all imperfections. "Progress is not an accident," said Spencer, "but a necessity. It is a part of Nature." And his American disciple, John Fiske, wrote raptly that "The creation of Man is the goal towards which Nature tended from the beginning. Not the production of any higher creature, but the perfecting of Humanity, is to be the glorious consummation of Nature's long and tedious work."

All this was gratifying enough, but as an explanation of history it is not very helpful. For to be told, when we ask why Rome declined or why the Spanish Armada foundered or why the Confederacy lost the Civil War, that it was all in harmony with the law of progress, or that it was part of evolution, leaves us pretty much where we were in the beginning. Granted progress, granted evolution, why should they manifest themselves in one way rather than in another? Was the decline of the Roman Empire progress? Is it certain that Britain and not Spain was destined to be the beneficiary of the evolutionary process?

No, the search for an explanation could not be satisfied that easily. If we were to explain the past, if we were to predict the future, we needed something at once more rigorous and more specific than the windy doctrine of progress or the impersonal doctrine of evolution. Mathematics, biology, chemistry, physics, these things had provided laws which explained so much that had heretofore been mysterious; surely history, too, could provide laws which would explain the past and illuminate the future. So said Auguste Comte, in France, who worked out an elaborate scheme of the social sciences; so said Herbert Spencer in England, who created a science of society on the basis of biology and anthropology and psychology; so said the American John Fiske whose *Outlines of Cosmic Philosophy* drew on the whole body of social and philosophical thought to find the laws which regulated the moral world, and whose many histories proved that these laws had operated in America from the beginning. Other social sciences boasted laws—Malthus' law of population growth, Gresham's law in economics, Ferdinand LaSalle's law of wages, Henry Buckle's law of geography, which was "one glorious principle of universal and undeviating regularity"—why should not history, too, have its laws?

Laws in History

"Four out of five students who are living today," wrote Henry Adams some sixty years ago,

> have, in the course of their work, felt that they stood on the brink of a great generalization that would reduce history under a law as clear as the laws which govern the material world ... He seemed to have it, as the Spanish say, in his ink stand. Scores of times he must have dropped his pen to think how one short step, one sudden inspiration, would show all human knowledge; how in these thickest forests of history, one corner turned, one faint trail struck, would bring him on the high road of science. [5]

Alas, when Adams himself hit on a law—it was the law of entropy, or the degradation of energy—it did not clear a way through thickest forests, but put up a permanent barrier to further historical research. Twenty years later Edward P. Cheyney sounded the same note:

I look forward [he said in his Presidential Address to the American Historical Association in 1923] to some future meeting of this Association when the search for the laws of History and their application will have become the principal part of their procedure ... The most conspicuous part on the program will be assigned to some gifted young historical thinker who, quite properly disregarding the earlier and crude efforts of his predecessors, will propound and demonstrate to the satisfaction of all his colleagues, some new and far-reaching law or laws of history.[6]

Alas, again, for human hopes; forty years later the sessions of the Historical Association were given over almost exclusively to "technical history," and philosophical speculations were looked upon with disfavor.

Professor Cheyney himself propounded six "laws of history" and it may be useful to recite them, for they reveal, as well as anything of their kind, some of the difficulties inherent in the formulation of such laws. They are (1) the law of continuity, (2) the law of mutability, (3) the law of interdependence, (4) the law of democracy, (5) the law of the necessity for free consent, and (6) the law of moral progress. Now it can be said of these—as of almost every attempt to formulate laws of history—that either they do not deal with history, but with life in general, or that they are not laws but expressions of hope and of faith. Take, for example, Cheyney's law of continuity. If this means that we have constructed a historical chronology and that in this chronology one event appears to follow another, then it is valid but meaningless. It means that everything that happens grows out of some antecedent cause which we can discover, then it is not so. The voyages of Columbus and the discovery of America doubtless grew out of complex antecedent causes which yield a logical pattern, but can it be said that the destruction of the Aztec and Incan empires grew out of recognizable causes and followed a pattern which the natives of Mexico and Peru would have regarded as logical? Scholars who trace the history of black slavery in America construct a neat and logical pattern, which almost makes us think that slavery was inevitable, but is there a comparable logic which would persuade Africans kidnapped and transported to America that slavery was inevitable for them? One major trouble with the principle of continuity and of causation is that it assumes a single line of continuity, a single chain of causes, instead of a hundred or a thousand.

Or consider Cheyney's law of mutability: that nothing is permanent in history. But that is not a law of history; it is a law of life, and poets and moralists had proclaimed it more than two thousand years before Cheyney took it over for history. What is important—and what the historian wants to know—is that some things appear to be more permanent than others. Which seem to be more permanent, and why? To this urgent question the law of mutability says nothing. It is as if we should submit, as a "law" of history, that all human beings are mortal and that all flesh is grass.

And what of Cheyney's other laws—democracy, liberty, morality? Clearly these are the formulations of a Victorian liberal. How many Chinese or Russian historians would subscribe to the "law" of democracy; how many American blacks would subscribe to the "law" of liberty; how many German Jews would endorse the "law" of moral progress, or for that matter, how many of the survivors of Hiroshima or of Dresden?

Confronted by the seemingly insuperable difficulty of formulating laws or solving the problems of causation, some historians have thrown in the sponge, as it were, and taken refuge in the principle of fortuity. Thus H. A. L. Fisher, whose *History of Europe* is something of a classic, confessed in his preface to that work that:

> One intellectual excitement has been denied me. Men wiser and more learned than I have discovered in history a plot, a rhythm, a predetermined pattern. These harmonies are concealed from me. I can see only one emergency following upon another as wave follows upon wave; only one great fact with respect to which, since it is unique, there can be no generalizations; only one safe rule for the historian: that he should recognize in the development of human destinies the play of the contingent and the unforeseen. [7]

In its most unsophisticated form this becomes the "Cleopatra's nose" theory of history first stated by no other than Blaise Pascal: "Had Cleopatra's nose been shorter, the whole face of the earth would have been different." Voltaire embraced the same theory, and so too did his friend Frederick the Great: "The older one becomes, the more clearly one sees that King Hazard fashions three-fourths of the events in this miserable world."

"The passion for tidiness," Arthur Schlesinger, Jr., has written, "is the historian's occupational disease." It is, indeed, though we should add in all fairness that it is a kind of historical necessity, as well. Organization always does some violence to the stream of thought or the chaos of conduct that is life—the organization of melody into music, the organization of color into painting, the organization of inspiration into poetry, and of ideas into philosophy, and the organization of facts into history. Granted that history is a record of disorderly conduct; it does not follow that it is to be reported in a disorderly fashion, and it is the mark of a great judge that he is able to bring order and coherence out of conflicting evidence and arguments. History is a jangle of accidents, blunders, surprises and absurdities, and so is our knowledge of it, but if we are to report it at all we must impose some order upon it. Literature is able to compensate for this necessity by falling back on the "stream of consciousness" technique, but history cannot do this.

The danger is that in tidying up history the historian will convey the impression (he may even convince himself!) that everything was tidy from the beginning. A battle, for example, is often a nightmare of blunder and confusion; then the historian comes along and tidies it all up, tells us just how the battle was planned, how the center struck at this moment and the left flank moved in next, how the artillery joined in, or the cavalry charged, and there is your victory, all nicely explained. Or he looks back upon a diplomatic incident, or upon an election, and explains it all very neatly, leaving out all the contingencies, all the unforeseen events, all the hesitations and fears and confusions. He presents us with the logic of some historical *fait accompli*—the Monroe Doctrine or the Open Door policy or Truman's Point Four, and we can indeed see how logical it all was; then we learn—as we have recently learned of Point Four, that it was all a series of accidents, and that far from being a deliberate policy it came even to President Truman himself as a happy surprise.

But while we must avoid assuming that history is a kind of chess game with every gambit logical and planned, we must avoid, equally, the other extreme, that of ascribing everything to accident or luck; we must avoid giving too much prominence to untidiness and disorder. For disorder is, in a sense, itself orderly; it is at once a principle of life and a rule of life. Birth is a very disorderly business, but we forget the disorder (or assume that it is taken for granted) and celebrate the birthday. The whole of life is disorderly—our growing-up, our education, our falling in love, our jobs or careers, our relations with friends or enemies. Our societies are disorderly—physically disorderly in their cities, institutionally disorderly in their economies, their politics, their social relationships. Intelligence tries to bring order out of all of this, and thereby to decrease the disorder, or to master it. So, too, in history, the intelligence of the historian is directed to bringing some order out of the chaos of the past.

And there is, too, a further and consoling consideration, that though accidents often change the pace or the pattern of history, they rarely change it in any fundamental way. For the sophisticated historian remembers what is, after all, the common sense of the matter, that there are always enough accidents to go around, and that accidents tend to cancel out, just as the sophisticated spectator at a football game knows that there are enough fumbles to go around and that a particular fumble rarely changes the course of a game, or of a season of games. It is immature and almost perverse to assign too much importance to what we denominate the accidents of history. The wind scattered the Spanish Armada and helped the English destroy it, but that was not the reason why Spain failed to conquer England; Spain had never conquered England, wind or no wind, nor had any other power. Washington surprised the Hessians at Trenton on Christmas of 1776, and the American cause looked up; but that was not the reason the Americans finally won their independence. Even had the Hessians repulsed Washington's ragged troops the Americans would, in all likelihood, have won sooner or later. A federal soldier picked up Lee's plan of battle for Antietam and took it to McClellan; that was not the reason Lee lost the battle of Antietam or the Confederacy lost the war. Even had Lee won the battle of Antietam it is highly improbable that the Confederacy would have won the war. President Wilson suffered a fateful breakdown on his train outside Wichita, Kansas, in the midst of his crusade for the ratification of the League of Nations, and the League was defeated. But that is not the reason that the Senate rejected the League or that the Republicans won the election of 1920; these things would have come about in any event, regardless of the fate of President Wilson.

Yet in every one of these instances, and in a hundred others which we could readily conjure up, fortuity did play a part, and an important part. It changed things; it meant that some people who might have lived, died; it meant that some battles had to be fought over again; it meant that what we call the course of history was slowed up or speeded up or temporarily deflected.

May we not conclude that fortuity itself is predictable, and that the mature historian takes it into account in his or her explanations, just as the wise general or statesman takes it into account in his calculations? An earthquake, a drought, the discovery of a new continent, or of gold and silver mines, an epidemic, an assassination, all of these are in a sense fortuitous, yet all of them are in a sense normal, as well, for such as these recur in the history of every country and every century.

Perhaps the most useful lesson the student of history can learn is to avoid oversimplification, and to accept the notion of multiple causation or to resign himself or herself to the fact that as yet we do not know enough to explain the causes of things. To yearn for a single, and usually simple, explanation of the chaotic materials of the past, to search for a single thread in that most tangled of all tangled skeins, is a sign of immaturity. More, it is a practice which encourages dangerous intellectual habits, for it leads, almost inevitably, to a simplistic view of the present as well as of the past. Any historian who invites us to accept some single explanation of the great events of the past excites our distrust; all too often such people find the explanation of prodigious events in some fortuitous occurrence, in some lurid conspiracy, or in some naive observation of character. They tell us that for want of a nail a kingdom was lost; they explain the Reformation in terms of Luther's desire to marry, or the Spanish conquest of Mexico in terms of Cortez' mistress.

The Philosophy of History

We come then, at the end, to the philosophy of history. The term itself is ambiguous. It may mean either one of two things, or both of them. It may mean the philosophy which the student brings to the study and the interpretation of history and to which he or she confidently expects history to conform. Or it may mean, more simply, the philosophy which the student finds in history, and to which the student will, perchance, conform.

The term *philosophy of history* is a formal and even a forbidding one. It conjures up for us those system makers and systems of the past, and of the present, too, who organized full-scale philosophies of history and demanded that history shoulder arms and march to its commands: an Augustine who proved that history was the working out of the will of God with man, a Hegel with his mystical sense of history as the history of freedom culminating in the present, a Condorcet who saw all history as a serried panorama of progress, a Karl Marx with his iron laws of history as a record of the struggle for material ends, a John Fiske with his assurance that history was progressive evolution, a Henry Adams imposing an irrelevant law of thermodynamics on the reluctant stuff of history, a Benedetto Croce with his magisterial principle that all history is contemporary history and must be recaptured and realized by each historian for himself, an Arnold Toynbee with his theory of the rise and dispersion of civilizations.

As we contemplate these and many other philosophies of history we are forced to conclude that the effort to compress the incalculably vast, infinitely complex, and wantonly elusive stuff of history into any single framework, or to express it in any single formula, is doomed to futility. This conclusion in turn suggests not so much that people have failed to solve the enigma of history as that there is no solution and possibly no enigma. Who are we, after all, to impose our will upon history? Who are we to require that it embrace our theories, dance to our tunes, march to our commands? Certainly nothing in the record of historical philosophy encourages us to believe that we can ever find some meaning in history upon which all sound people will agree.

Indeed the very multiplicity of historical philosophies and the inability of the most profound historians to agree on the meaning of history suggest that the philosophies are dictated not by history itself, but by circumstances, or by the temperament and the training of the historical philosophers.

All of this is entirely natural. After all, philosophers and saints have been brooding over the relation of man to God for thousands of years without arriving at a common religion. Philosophers and statesmen have been working out political theories for over two thousand years without arriving at one on which any large portion of humankind voluntarily agrees. Philosophers and teachers have been considering the nature of education for centuries, but we have not yet arrived at any generally accepted philosophy of education. Why should we expect an authoritative philosophy of history when we still lack authoritative philosophies of religion, politics, or education?

If the deductive approach to the philosophy of history is unprofitable, let us turn to the inductive. G. M. Trevelyan has well said that philosophy is not something you take to history, it is something you carry away from history. If we cannot impose our philosophical patterns upon history, let us see if history can impose philosophical lessons upon us.

This is, to be sure, a manner of speech. There is no such thing as "history" in the abstract, something which works out lessons and proceeds to impose them upon its disciples. What we mean when we say that "history" imposes its lessons is that after prolonged study and profound consideration of some chapter of history, the historian, like the educator, or the jurisprudent, or the political philosopher, may draw some general conclusions about its meaning, its purposes, and its value. Such considerations will have no scientific validity; they will have only the authority which may attach itself to the character and the reputation of the historian. But that is true in every nonscientific domain. If, over the years and centuries, learned and sagacious scholars from many different societies arrive at some common generalizations, may we not be justified in according these some degree of respect?

So, at least, men have thought in the past. "The great errors of the age are very useful," wrote Voltaire. "One cannot remind oneself too often of crimes and disasters. These, no matter what people say, can be forestalled. The history of the tyrant Christiern can prevent a nation from giving absolute power to a tyrant, and the undoing of Charles XII at Pultawa will warn a generation not to plunge too deeply into the Ukraine without supplies." That is combining the serious and the frivolous with a vengeance, but is suggests how the liveliest mind of the eighteenth century turned to history, and wrote it, too. Certainly the American Founding Fathers thought the study of history profitable. All of them were immersed in history, especially in the history of the ancient world; almost all of them wrote history. They drew with confidence on the history of the past to justify independence, to guide them along the paths of federalism, to provide examples for their every experiment in politics and government, to illuminate the problem of the reconciliation of liberty and order. The debates in the Federal Convention of 1787, the debates in the ratifying conventions, *The Federalist* papers—these are one continuous historical commentary. And so, too, the private letters of John Adams, Madison, Jefferson, Hamilton, Washington—it was always history they turned to, for examples and illustrations and morals. Nor were the resources of history exhausted with the ratification of the Constitution. Washington drew upon history when he warned his fellow countrymen against the baleful influences of factions and parties; Jefferson called upon it when he denounced the Alien and Sedition Acts and celebrated the long record of freedom from governmental tyranny; Calhoun invoked it to vindicate states' rights, and Webster, in that eloquent appeal for a Union one and inseparable, which still has the power to quicken our heartbeats. Lincoln reviewed the history of the nation in his first inaugural address to prove that "the nation came before the states," and he began his Gettysburg Address with a reminder of what had happened four score and seven years ago. —A hundred other examples flood into our minds; it is sufficient to recall one of the most fateful. Winston Churchill, a historian as well as a maker of history, tells us that when at Chequers he heard the news of the attack on

Pearl Harbor, he knew that Britain was saved. "I had studied the American Civil War, fought out to the last desperate inch...I went to bed and slept the sleep of the saved."

We have quoted before what is probably the most familiar of all definitions of history: "philosophy teaching by examples." The phrase is Bolingbroke's, but Dionysius of Halicarnassus said the same thing two thousand years ago, and fifteen centuries later, Sir Walter Raleigh, who was a historian as well as an explorer, wrote that "the end and scope of all history" is "to teach us by examples of times past such wisdom as may guide our desires and actions." No definition is more hackneyed; perhaps none is more acceptable.

Very well, then; if history is philosophy teaching by examples, what does it teach?

Candor forces us to confess that it teaches pretty much what historians or, more commonly, those who are in power, want taught. All too often, over the centuries, history has been the camp follower of victorious armies, the champion of successful parties, the apologist of dominant classes, the protagonist of established religions. Indeed, so widespread is the exploitation of history for personal, partisan, religious, class, or national purposes, that we cannot but have some sympathy with Napoleon's remark that "history is a lie agreed upon," or with Matthew Arnold's reference to "that huge Mississippi of falsehood called history," or speculate how applicable to history is Justice Holmes' sardonic definition of truth: "the majority vote of that nation that can lick all others." How sobering it is that in almost every major war both sides have invoked history with complete assurance that it will respond. Over the years history has been made to do service for almost every cause. The rich and the powerful on both sides of the Atlantic invoked the history of the French Revolution to damn all popular reforms and protect their privileges. Southern planters used the history of Greece and Rome to prove that slavery was a beneficent institution, and essential to a high civilization. Hitler prostituted history to prove the superiority of the Aryans over all other races. The Chinese Communists today rewrite history to prove that the white races have always exploited the yellow. Even in smaller matters politicians do not hesitate to summon up history to vindicate their arguments: that inflation always leads to ruin, or that centralization inevitably leads to tyranny, or that socialization destroys initiative, or that the majority have a peculiar proclivity for injustice.

If this were the whole story, we might well conclude that the study of history was at best an idle self-indulgence, and at worst corrupting; a number of critics have come to just that conclusion—Nietzsche and Verlaine among them. Happily it is not the whole story. History has other and more benevolent uses. It can, and does, provide humankind with memory. It does fire the imagination, broaden intellectual horizons, and deepen sympathies. It does summon up a great cloud of witnesses from the past to instruct and edify each new generation. It does encourage each generation to believe that it can build upon the past and perhaps progress into the future. And it does inculcate moral precepts.

What moral precepts? History provides perspective. It reminds us that time is indeed long and our own life fleeting; that for thousands of years each generation has thought that it was the end and the object of history; that people have known crises before, and wars, and turmoils, and triumph and tragedy, and have survived; that those issues and problems which loom so large on our horizons may not even be visible on the larger horizon of history; and that the cloud-capp'd towers, the gorgeous palaces, the solemn temples, which to us seem the very wonders of the world, may dissolve and leave not a rack behind.

Because history gives us a larger perspective, it moderates our instinctive and pervasive parochialism, a parochialism of both time and space, a parochialism which is moral as well as social or political. It teaches us that the world is large, miscellaneous, and haphazard, not subject to our fiat or to our desires. It tells us that one people and then another, one nation and then another, one civilization and then another has moved to the center of the historical stage, and claimed for itself the principal role, and then moved into the shadows. It admonishes us that our habits and interests, our standards and values, have no cosmic validity; that we cannot impose our will upon history, or bestride history like some Colossus. It teaches therefore modesty and humility.

Along with these precepts history enjoins patience—patience with the long struggle of humans to conquer nature, to organize government and society, to cope with the thousand problems that glare and glower upon them ceaselessly through time. It teaches patience with the errors of humans, the mischief of their enterprises, the failures of their institutions, the frustrations of their hopes and ambitions. It teaches patience too with our own contemporaries, patience with those who, in the words of Jefferson describing the French Revolution, "seek through blood and slaughter their long-lost liberties"; patience with those who are just now emerging out of centuries of darkness and deprivation and are trying to catch up, in one convulsive leap, with the peoples of the Western world; patience with those who do not accept or adopt our ways of thinking or adopt our institutions; patience with experiments that seem misguided and even pernicious. It counsels us to be patient with the unfathomable processes of history, the unexpected, the unforeseen, the unfamiliar; with change that never comes the way we want it to come; with problems that are never solved the way we would solve them, or that are simply transformed into new problems equally insoluble. It teaches us patience with all of this, but impatience with all those simplifications which do violence to the mysterious complexity, the subtlety, the richness and density and intricacy of the historical process.

History teaches tolerance—tolerance with different faiths, different loyalties, different cultures, different ideas and ideals. It instructs us that over the centuries there have been so many of these, so many faiths, so many cultures, so many nations, so many parties, so many philosophies, that each people has been guilty of supposing, "Lo we are the people and all wisdom dies with us"; that each sect, each party, has indulged in the vanity of believing that it, somehow, represented the larger purposes of history and the will of God. It teaches tolerance of alien peoples and opposing interests, and of ideas which, in the words of Justice Holmes, we think "loathsome and fraught with death." It teaches. therefore, the necessity of freedom—freedom for inquiry, freedom for heterodoxy and dissent—for it makes clear that freedom is the only method humankind has thus far found for avoiding error and discovering truth.

History assures us that people are neither the creatures of iron laws over which they have no control nor the victims of chance and fortuity. They need not sink beneath some secular determinism, nor need they acquiesce in the notion that day after day the wind of history bloweth where it listeth, and that they are the sports of vagrant historical winds. For history tells us that if people are not masters of their fate, neither are they the victims of fate. It reminds us, by a thousand stirring examples, that the individual counts, that character counts. It makes clear that it was the genius of Mohammed that revitalized the Arab world, that it was the moral power of the Maid of Orleans which united the French against the English; that the iron will of Cromwell was essential to the triumph of the Puritan cause; that it was Washington who made possible the American victory in the Revolutionary War, that Mahatma Gandhi was the driving force behind Indian independence and nationhood, and that without Winston Churchill's eloquence and resolution, England might have gone under before help could have arrived from across the sea.

And does not history tell us, too, that it is not only the character of the individual but of a whole people that counts? "What kind of a people do they think we are?" cried Churchill at a famous moment in history, and may we not say that it was because Hitler and his supporters were ignorant and contemptuous of history that they failed so fatefully to understand what kind of people the Bristish were. The character of a people counts, and makes a difference — in the long nightmare struggle of the Dutch against their Spanish overlords, in the bulldog tenacity of the British against the Napoleonic imperium, in the passionate patriotism and courage of the Swiss, in the courage, the prudence, the industry, the wisdom of the Norwegians in surviving through Nazi tyranny and rebuilding their shattered nation after liberation.

And history reminds us, too, that character is to be read not only in manifestations of courage and power, but in things of the mind and the spirit as well. We do not turn to the histories of ancient Athens, of Renaissance Florence and Siena, of Elizabethan England or colonial Virginia or nineteenth-century Denmark because they recount great deeds of courage or mighty strokes of power, but because they provide us with refreshment of the mind and the spirit. History admonishes us that the tests of happiness, of greatness, and of power are not everywhere or always the same, and that in the long run, what we turn to are not the triumphs of wealth and of might but of the mind and the spirit of humankind.

It is not given us to know the causes of things, but the search for causes is itself an affluent enterprise, one which enlarges the mind and quickens the sympathies of all who engage in it. No laws of history command authority, but the study of those manifold forces which ceaselessly play upon history deepens our understanding and brings magnanimity to our judgment. No philosophy encompasses or explains the trackless course of history, but to those who study it with sympathy and understanding and imagination, history teaches philosophy. *Esto perpetuo.*

Notes

1. George Macaulay Trevelyan, *Clio, A Muse, and Other Essays* (London: Longmans, Green, 1913), p.26.
2. George Macaulay Trevelyan, *Critical Essays,* p.4.
3. Emerson, Divinity School Address, 15 July 1838.

4. Henry Adams, *The Education of Henry Adams* (Boston: Houghton Mifflin Co., 1918), p. 484.
5. Ibid.
6. Edward P. Cheyney, *Law in History and Other Essays* (New York: Alfred A. Knopf, 1927).
7. H. A. L. Fisher, *A History of Europe* (Boston: Houghton Mifflin Co., 1935—36), preface.

Bibliography

Acton, Lord. *Essays on Freedom and Power.* Edited by Gertrude Himmelfarb. Boston: Beacon Press, 1948.

Ausubel, Herman. *Historians and Their Craft: A Study of the Presidential Addresses to the American Historical Association, 1884-1945.* New York: Columbia University Press, 1952.

———et al. *Some Modern Historians of Britain, Essays in Honor of R. L. Schuyler.* New York: Holt, Rinehart and Winston, 1951.

Barraclough, Geoffrey. *History in a Changing World.* New York: Oxford University Press, 1955.

Barzun, Jacques, and Graff, Henry A. *The Modern Researcher.* New York: Harcourt, Brace & World, 1957.

Bassett, John Spencer. *The Middle Group of American Historians.* New York: The Macmillan Co., 1947.

Beard, Charles A. *The Economic Basis of Politics.* New York: Random House, 1957.

Becker, Carl. *Everyman His Own Historian.* New York: Appleton-Century-Crofts, 1935.

Benson, Lee. *Toward the Scientific Study of History: Selected Essays.* Philadelphia: J. B. Lippincott, 1972.

Beringer, Richard E. *Historical Analysis: Contemporary Approaches to Clio's Craft.* New York: Wiley, 1978.

Berkhofer, Robert F. *A Behavioral Approach to Historical Analysis.* New York: The Free Press, 1969.

Berlin, Isaiah. *Historical Inevitability.* New York: Oxford University Press, 1954.

Bloch, Marc. *The Historian's Craft.* New York: Alfred A. Knopf, 1953.

Bogue, Allan G., ed. *Emerging Theoretical Models in Social and Political History.* Beverly Hills: Sage Publications, 1973.

Bowen, Catherine Drinker. *Adventures of a Biographer.* Boston: Atlantic-Little, Brown, 1959.

Bury, J. B. *The Ancient Greek Historians.* New York: The Macmillan Co., 1909.

———. *The Idea of Progress.* New York: The Macmillan Co., 1932.

Butterfield, Herbert. *The Englishman and His History.* Cambridge: Cambridge University Press, 1944.

———. *History and Human Relations.* London: Collins, 1951.

———. *Man on His Past: The Study of the History of Historical Scholarship.* Cambridge: Cambridge University Press, 1954.

Carr, Edward Hallett. *What Is History?* New York: Alfred A. Knopf, 1962.

Cartwright, William H., and Watson, Richard L., Jr. *The Reinterpretation of American History and Culture.* Washington: National Council for the Social Studies, 1973.

Cassirer, Ernst. *The Philosophy of the Enlightenment.* Boston: Beacon Press, 1951.

Cheyney, Edward P. *Law in History and Other Essays.* New York: Alfred A. Knopf, 1927.

Collingwood, R. G. *The Idea of History.* Oxford: Clarendon Press, 1946.

Dilthey, Wilhelm. *Pattern and Meaning in History.* New York: Harper & Row, 1961.

Dollar, Charles M., and Jensen, Richard J. *Historian's Guide to Statistics: Quantitative Analysis and Historical Research.* New York: Holt, Rinehart and Winston, 1971.

Dunning, William A. *Truth in History and Other Essays.* Introduction by J. G. DeRoulhac Hamilton. New York: Columbia University Press, 1937.

Flint, Robert. *History of the Philosophy of History.* Edinburgh and London: William Blackwood and Sons, 1893.

Gardiner, Patrick, ed. *Theories of History: Readings from Classical and Contemporary Sources.* New York: Free Press of Glencoe, 1959.

Geyl, Pieter. *Debates with Historians.* Cleveland: The World Publishing Co., 1958.

———. *Encounters in History.* New York: Meridian Books, 1961.

Gooch, G. P. *History and Historians in the Nineteenth Century.* 2d ed. New York: David McKay Co., 1952.

Gottschalk, Louis. *Generalization in the Writing of History.* Chicago: The University of Chicago Press, 1963.

———. *Understanding History.* New York: Alfred A. Knopf, 1950.

Harrison, Frederic. *The Meaning of History.* New York: The Macmillan Co., 1908.

Hexter, J. H. *Reappraisals in History.* Evanston, Ill.: Northwestern University Press, 1961.

Higham, John. *Writing American History: Essays on Modern Scholarship.* Bloomington: Indiana University Press, 1970.

Hofstadter, Richard. *The Progressive Historians: Turner, Beard, Parrington.* New York: Alfred A. Knopf, 1968.

Hughes, H. Stuart. *History as Art and as Science.* New York: Harper & Row, 1964.

Hutchinson, William T., ed. *The Marcus W. Jerregan Essays in American Historiography.* Chicago: University of Chicago Press, 1937.

Kabler, Eric. *The Meaning of History.* New York: George Braziller, 1964.

Kent, Sherman. *Writing History.* New York: Appleton-Century-Crofts, 1941.

Kichan, Lionel. *Action on History.* London: Deutsch, 1954.

Klibansky, Raymond, and Paton, H. J., eds. *Philosophy and History.* New York, Evanston, and London: Harper & Row, 1963.

Knowles, Davis. *The Historian and Character.* Cambridge: Cambridge University Press, 1963.

Kraus, Michael. *A History of American History.* New York: Farrar and Rinehart, 1937.

Laistner, M. L. W. *The Greater Roman Historians.* Berkeley: University of California Press, 1947.

Leisy, Ernest E. *The American Historical Novel.* Norman, Okla.: University of Oklahoma Press, 1950.

Levin, David. *History as Romantic Art: Bancroft, Prescott, Motley, and Parkman.* Stanford, Calif.: Stanford University Press, 1959.

Lovejoy, Arthur O. *Essays in the History of Ideas.* Baltimore: Johns Hopkins University Press, 1948.

Malin, James. *The Contriving Brain and the Skillful Hand in the United States: Something About History and the Philosophy of History.* Lawrence, Kan.: University of Kansas Press, 1955.

_____. *Essays on Historiography.* Lawrence, Kan.: University of Kansas Press, 1946.

_____. *On the Nature of History: Essays about History and Dissidence.* Lawrence, Kan.: University of Kansas Press, 1954.

Meyerhoff, Hans. *The Philosophy of History in Our Time: An Anthology Selected and Edited by Hans Meyerhoff.* Garden City, N. Y.: Doubleday & Co., 1959.

Morison, Samuel Eliot. *Vistas of History.* New York: Alfred A. Knopf, 1964.

Muller, Herbert J. *The Uses of the Past.* New York: Columbia University Press, 1952.

Namier, L. B. *Avenues of History.* London: Hamish Hamilton, 1952.

Neff, Emery. *The Poetry of History.* New York: Columbia University Press, 1947.

Nevins, Allan. *The Gateway to History.* Garden City, N. Y.: Doubleday & Co., 1962.

_____. "Not Capulets, Not Montagus," *American Historical Review* 65 (1960): 253-71.

Niebuhr, Reinhold. *The Irony of American History.* New York: Charles Scribner's Sons, 1952.

Nietzsche, Friedrich. *The Use and Abuse of History.* New York: Liberal Arts Press, 1949.

Pares, Richard. *The Historian's Business and Other Essays.* Edited by R. A. Humphreys and Elisabeth Humphreys. New York: Oxford University Press, 1961.

Popper, Karl. *The Poverty of Historicism.* Boston: Beacon Press, 1957.

Renier, Gustaf J. *History, Its Purpose and Method.* Boston: Beacon Press, 1950.

Rowse, A. L. *The Use of History.* New York: The Macmillan Co., 1947.

Salmon, Lucy M. *Why Is History Rewritten?* Introduction by Edward P. Cheyney. New York: Oxford University Press, 1929.

Schevill, Ferdinand. *Six Historians.* Chicago: University of Chicago Press, 1956.

Siracusa, Joseph M. *New Left Diplomatic Histories and Historians: The American Revisionists.* Port Washington, N. Y.: Kennikut Press, 1973.

Smith, Page. *The Historian and History.* New York: Alfred A. Knopf, 1964.

Stern, Fritz, ed. *Varieties of History.* New York: Meridian Books, 1956.

Strayer, Joseph R., ed. *The Interpretation of History.* Princeton, N. J.: Princeton University Press, 1943.

Strout, Cushing. *The Pragmatic Revolt in American History: Carl Becker and Charles Beard.* New Haven, Conn.: Yale University Press, 1958.

Teggart, Frederick J. *The Processes of History.* New Haven, Conn.: Yale University Press, 1948.

_____. *Prolegomena to History: The Relation of History to Literature, Philosophy, and Science.* Berkeley: University of California Press, 1916.

_____. *Theory and Processes of History.* Berkeley: University of California Press, 1941.

Thompson, J. W. *A History of Historical Writing.* New York: The Macmillan Co., 1942.

Trevelyan, George Macaulay. *Clio, a Muse, and Other Essays.* London: Longmans, Green, 1913. 2d ed., 1930.

_____. *An Autobiography and Other Essays.* London: Longmans, Green, 1949.

Wedgwood, C. V. *The Sense of the Past.* New York: Columbia University Press, 1957.

————. *Truth and Opinion.* New York: The Macmillan Co., 1960.

Weiss, Paul. *History, Written and Lived.* Carbondale, Ill.: Southern Illinois University Press, 1962.

Wish, Harvey. *The American Historian.* New York: Oxford University Press, 1960.

————, ed. *American Historians, A Selection.* New York: Oxford University Press, 1962.

six

Suggested Methods for Teachers

Raymond H. Muessig

... When we estrange ourselves from history we do not enlarge, we diminish ourselves, even as individuals. We subtract from our lives one meaning which they do in fact possess, whether we recognize it or not. We cannot help living in history. We can only fail to be aware of it. If we are to meet, endure, and transcend the trials and defeats of the future—for trials and defeats there are certain to be—it can only be from a point of view which, seeing the future as part of the sweep of history, enables us to establish our place in that immense procession in which is incorporated whatever hope humankind may have. (Robert L. Heilbroner, *The Future as History*)[1]

Introduction

Dr. Commager has dedicated this book to Allan Nevins, whose writing I have long appreciated. In one of my favorite works by Nevins, *The Gateway to History,* he wrote, "History is any integrated narrative, description or analysis of past events or facts written in a spirit of *critical inquiry* for the whole truth."[2] In *Truth and Opinion: Historical Essays,* C. V. Wedgwood observed that "If history is educational—and I have a vested interest in believing it to be so—it must be an education in *thinking* not merely in remembering."[3] And in *History As Art and As Science,* H. Stuart Hughes said that merely "to identify something—to label it accurately or to locate it in chronological sequence—is not to *know* it in the historian's usual meaning of the term. Historical knowledge involves *meaning*"; Hughes continued by defining "meaning" as "the connectedness of things."[4]

A major purpose of this chapter is to suggest methods that could make history more meaningful to elementary and secondary students. I also hope that the instructional strategies and media proposed will make the teaching and learning of social studies in general and of history in particular increasingly interesting, individualized, humane, varied, challenging, enriching, and enjoyable.

Helping Students to Examine the Whys and Wherefores of History

In his preface, Dr. Commager restates questions some historians have addressed to themselves increasingly the past hundred years or so regarding the nature of history, its pursuits, possibilities, and problems. Although I had read a little philosophy of history and historiography prior to 1957, it was in September of that year that a ninth grader in one of my classes of "Backgrounds of Western Civilization" stimulated me to think at a practical, methodological level about an issue on which I have since continued to deliberate. Without warning, the student fired at me, "Why do we have to study this stuff?!"

That evening, I mapped out my first teaching strategy designed to get pupils to consider history as such. Having gathered hundreds of quotations and aphorisms on numerous and diverse topics for years, I started with a rough idea the following day in class. I continued thereafter to try different things around definitions and observations associated with Clio, and the rest—excuse the poor pun—is history.

The secondary classroom teacher who is confronted with "Why do we have to study history?" or who wishes to initiate such an examination, might convert the question into an open, genuine reflective issue: Should people study history?

The teacher could announce that he or she is going to "sponsor a contest." A hamburger, a soft drink, and fries would be awarded to three winners, with all class members and the teacher having a chance to vote. A prize would go to the student with the best reasons in favor of the study of history. As a way of provoking the "enemy forces" into exhausting their supply of ammunition, the teacher would feed the person who most effectively opposes the study of history. In the best "reflective" tradition, "junk food" would be purchased as well for the scholar with the most, the best, and the best-balanced arguments on why history should and should not be studied.

To launch independent reading, research, deliberation, and writing, the teacher might provide each pupil with a duplicated handout composed of sequential learning activities. First, each participant could be asked to read and to ponder a list of quotations related to the nature, study, positive and negative attributes, and possible overtones of history, such as these:

> "Those who cannot remember the past are condemned to repeat it." —*George Santayana*
> "Certainly, even if history were judged incapable of other uses, its entertainment value would remain in its favor."—*Marc Bloch*
> "Anything but history, for history must be false." —*Sir Robert Walpole*
> "History makes us some amends for the shortness of life." —*Philip Skelton*

"One age cannot be completely understood if all the others are not understood. The song of history can only be sung as a whole." —*José Ortega y Gasset*

"Histories make men wise." —*Sir Francis Bacon*

"I tell you the past is a bucket of ashes." —*Carl Sandburg*

"History approaches closer to everyday experience than any other branch of knowledge." —*H. Stuart Hughes*

"History is simply a piece of paper covered with print; the main thing is still to make history, not to write it." —*Otto von Bismarck-Schönhausen*

"As a result of studying history, people occasionally stumble on the truth; but they almost always get up and continue on their way as if nothing had happened." —*Anonymous*

"History is the cognitive expression of the deep-rooted human desire to know the past which, in a spontaneous untutored way, is born afresh with every child that searched the mystery of its being. History springs from a live concern, deals with life, serves life." —*Fritz Stern*

"History is little more than the register of crimes and misfortunes." —*François Marie Arouet Voltaire*

"Life must be lived forwards, but can only be understood backwards." —*Sören Aabye Kierkegaard*

"Not to know what has been transacted in former times is to be always a child." —*Marcus Tullius Cicero*

"History is the science of what never happens twice." —*Paul Valery*

"[It] is impossible to divorce history from life: Mr. Everyman can not do what he needs or desires to do without recalling past events; he can not recall past events without in some subtle fashion relating them to what he needs or desires to do." —*Carl L. Becker*

"History is more or less bunk." —*Henry Ford*

["History is] the rival of time, the depository of great actions, the witness of what is past, the example and instruction of the present, the monitor of the future." —*Miguel de Cervantes*

"History never embraces more than a small part of reality." —*François de La Rouchefoucauld*

"Nothing changes more constantly than the past; for the past that influences our lives does not consist of what actually happened, but of what men believe happened." —*Gerald White Johnson*

"Peoples and governments have never learned anything from history, or acted upon principles deducible from it." —*Georg Wilhelm Friedrich Hegel*

"It is very difficult to trace and find out the truth of anything by history." —*Plutarch*

"What is past is prologue." —*William Shakespeare*

The second step in this recommended procedure could be to encourage every learner to select one of the quotations from the teacher's list or to locate still another intriguing passage. The student could be asked to write the actual quotation chosen on the top of a lined piece of paper. Next, the class member might be challenged to write the given excerpt in his or her own words in a brief, clear form. (Students need practice in paraphrasing passages, and by checking the restatements, the teacher could assist participants in clarifying any possible misunderstandings regarding the intended meaning of an author.) Fourth, every individual could explain why he or she agrees or disagrees with the quotation that has been reworded. Then, moving to a more general level, everyone could be requested to explain in writing what he or she thinks are some of the appeals, positive features, and strengths of history and its study. The sixth stage would be for the pupil to treat what he or she believes are certain of the drawbacks, negative features, and weaknesses of history and its study.

Seventh, the class member might attempt to list some of the things likely to happen in the future—both the short- and the long-range consequences—if his or her beliefs regarding history were to be taken seriously and acted on personally and/or by others on a broader scale.

At the eighth—and best—stage, the teacher could urge each class member to create his or her own "quotable quote," expressing his or her views on history as precisely, succinctly, persuasively, imaginatively, and/or humorously as possible. To his or her literary skill, every learner might then add his or her artistic talents by lettering and illustrating the quotation for display on the classroom bulletin boards or walls. (The name of each author-artist would not appear on the work at this time, but the student's contribution would be kept on display and identified later by a little "museum tag," printed and posted by the teacher or one of the class members.) Ninth, each pupil could read and take notes on his or her classmates' sayings to gain additional and varied points of view. Next, for the "contest," every person should be ready to compose his or her essay—ranging, perhaps, from 100 to 200 words—on arguments *for, against,* or *for and against* the study of history. All the essays could then be typed, duplicated, stapled in complete sets, and distributed throughout the class so that every person's position statement could be read, assessed, and voted on. Twelfth, the votes would be tabulated, the three "champions" announced, and arrangements made for the teacher to treat the winners!

Introducing and Reinforcing Understandings and Skills Related to Chronological Sequence

In a chapter entitled "The Sweep of the Narrative Line," a professor of European history concludes that it is *"chronological sequence that most sharply distinguishes the writing of history from all other intellectual pursuits."* [5] *History*—one of the books in *Humanistic Scholarship in America: The Princeton Studies*— written by John Higham, with Leonard Krieger and Felix Gilbert, calls attention to everyone's "constant need to remember the jumble of experience in *orderly sequence. . . . "* [6] The activities suggested in this section are developmental in character, moving from the first planned learning experiences with chronological sequence for children in the primary grades on up through more complex and abstract approaches appropriate for adolescents and young adults. A well-established foundation with respect to chronological sequence is important and helpful, for it nourishes and correlates nicely with other logical, linear thought patterns and with causation and, later, multiple causation.

As part of a field trip to a farm for various purposes, the second or third grade teacher could help his or her charges see and talk about various kinds of animals at different stages of development. For instance, the teacher and room parents might guide small groups of boys and girls through careful observation first of the gathering of newly laid eggs, then of eggs in an incubator, next of baby chicks emerging from their shells, and so on to mature chickens. Or, a thoroughly preplanned excursion to a clean, reputable kennel could be enlightening and enjoyable. There, children might see a tiny, newborn Dalmatian—which appears to be white—and then, looking at progressively older examples of the breed, witness the miraculous process by which the beautiful creatures acquire silver, light gray, gray, and finally black spots as they age from puppies to dogs.

Or, the teacher might plan a simple afternoon party, when the whole class would greet five to eight guests of different ages. The visitors could include a baby and a young child, a fifth or sixth grader in the same school, an eighth or ninth grader in a nearby junior high school, a high school senior, a person 30 to 50, and an individual over 65. The teacher would have secured brief information on each guest (name, age, place of birth, current activities, interests), which would have been printed clearly on a lined 4" × 6" card. Pupils who volunteer, or whose names are drawn from a shoe box containing a slip of paper identifying every class member, get to introduce the visitors, either reading from the cards or using the information as a guide for a less formal approach. In advance, the teacher would have cut 9" × 9" pieces of colored poster board. On each square, the teacher would paint a large number, from 1 to however many guests have been invited. Putting a small hole in each side of the top of every square, the teacher would thread through and tie a piece of string long enough to slip over each visitor's head. (The person holding the baby would wear the infant's card.) Next, the guests would be asked to stand in the front of the room, in *no special order.* The visitors would be introduced at this point. Then the teacher would challenge the class to place the guests in line, from the youngest on up to the oldest, hanging the lowest number on the youngest person and the highest number on the oldest individual. Class volunteers would be invited to come up to a visitor, *to place the guest in the correct sequence,* and to put a numbered card over the visitor's head. The volunteers could start from either direction, and it is likely that the baby and the senior citizen would be located early at the opposite ends of the line. The teacher could pretend to *try* to keep everyone absolutely quiet until all the guests are standing someplace in line and wearing a number, but there would probably be considerable whispering and meaningful interaction as boys and girls try to help each other with hints. Many class members might not have listened well to the introductions and might not have caught the visitors' ages; so some adjustments in the placement of guests could be necessary. A general class discussion could be held at this point until pupils are satisfied with the sequential arrangement of the visitors. The teacher might help the children to summarize and to generalize insights gained from this strategy. At this stage, the teacher could shift from a total class endeavor to committees of three to five learners, so that more interaction could take place and so that he or she could move frequently from group to group, see how pupils are progressing, and assist with questions and suggestions.

Remembering that helping boys and girls understand and apply their understanding of the idea of chronological sequence is the major purpose here—not dealing with specific names, dates, places, events, etc., as such in history—the primary teacher might decide to blend in an added dash of science and foster a broader application of sequence by using the life cycles of interesting and varied plants and animals to give children some practice. The teacher might gather reproductions of drawings, paintings, lithographs, and photographs from post cards, calendars, magazines, picture books, and discussion series of representative flowers, trees, insects, spiders, fish, amphibians, reptiles, birds, and mammals. Specific examples could suggest committees' names, such as *Easter Lily, Maple Tree, Monarch Butterfly, Black Widow Spider, Salmon, Leopard Frog, Painted Turtle, Barn Swallow,* and *Wallaroo Kangaroo.* Each of four to six pictures would show one of the stages in the development of the flora and fauna. The illustrations for a subject (say, the monarch butterfly) would be displayed initially in incorrect order (e.g., larva, adult, egg, pupa), and committee members would do their best to think through a possible sequence

Figure 1.

and to work out a brief "life story" that one representative could tell to the entire class when everyone has reassembled. While one child talks, others in his or her group could hold up the appropriate illustrations. A report might sound something like this:

> We had a frog. That was easy, 'cause last year we saw the whole thing in Mr. Hall's second grade. The pitcher of the egg has to come first. Then a tadpole in an egg. After that, just a tadpole. Next, a tadpole with legs. Then a frog. Right?

Each oral report could be followed by questions and comments from the class and the teacher, and any sequential errors would be discussed and corrected. Having planned learning experiences on chronological sequence for the class as a whole and for the children in groups, the teacher might want to develop an individual activity to reinforce learning and to evaluate the growth of each learner. This time the teacher could use photographs taken of one person over a period of years. Just for fun, the teacher could be the subject, selecting five to ten photos of himself or herself from such sources as a baby book, family and personal snapshots, professional prints, school pictures at different levels, a wedding album, and so on. Or, the teacher might borrow ten to fifteen photos of an older relative, friend, or neighbor. Again, the illustrations would be displayed initially in incorrect chronological order, as seen in figure 1. The teacher could sit beside each individual class member and ask the second or third grader to talk aloud about what he or she is thinking as he or she is arranging the photographs from youngest to oldest, earliest to latest. At first, the teacher might be as "nondirective" as possible, answering the pupil's questions with questions and letting the boy or girl get off to a slow start, engage in trial-and-error behavior for awhile, and make mistakes. In time, however, the teacher would help the learner to refine his or her thinking about chronological sequence.

Children who have had experiences with chronological sequence such as the preceding can be moved easily into a form of activity that can be adapted meaningfully for use all of the way from the third or fourth grade on through every level to and beyond the twelfth grade. This teaching method involves the use of earlier-to-later photographs of a variety of subjects, such as fashions, recreational activities, holiday celebrations, occupations, tools, weapons, construction techniques, forms of housing, roads, bridges, dams, boats, trains, tractors, automobiles, aircraft, beds, household appliances, writing and printing equipment, forms of communication, and medical and dental practices. Figure 2 illustrates some of the endless possibilities at a few different conceptual levels, and, again, the pictures have been put in improper order, as they would be placed initially before learners of various ages. All the examples in figure 2 are copy stand shots from photographs in the interesting and varied collection to which I was directed by understanding, helpful, imaginative, courteous professionals at the Ohio Historical Society. The enterprising elementary or secondary teacher—with a little knowledge of photography, or with a friend, a fellow teacher, or a school or district instructional media director who has the equipment and know-how for copy work—can secure permission to photograph fascinating old-to-new photographs found in museums, libraries, archives, books, magazines, and picture albums. Photos can be printed in the same size and mounted on heavy cardboard or blocks of wood for easy manipulation by learners. Of course, once the teacher (or the school or the district) has a collection of photographs such as those in figure 2, the pictures can be used to teach and to give pupils practice with chronological sequence in innumerable ways.

Figure 2.

Figure 2 *(Continued)*

For instance, with boys and girls between grades four and seven, the teacher could have thirty sets of four to six prints. Each set would be on a different topic, such as photographs of the same street corner taken at twenty-year intervals, of a crystal set on up through a pocket radio, or of a university from the first building to a much later aerial shot of the campus with many structures. The desks in the classroom would be spaced as widely apart as possible and would be lined up in rows. Each desk would be used as a station, with one set of photographs displayed in improper order on it. Another class in the school would be invited to "man" the desks, to tabulate the correct and incorrect arrangements of each set of photographs, and to scramble the pictures after every round. The teacher might "ham" this approach up even more by using a stopwatch and a buzzer or a kitchen timer with a bell. The idea would be to have fun and to keep things moving. Class members would have only one minute at each station. In a little more than a half hour, therefore, they would arrange all thirty sets of photographs in what they believe to be the correct chronological sequence. Each tabulator from the visiting class would have the number of his or her set of historical photographs at the top of a sheet of paper divided into two columns marked "right" and "wrong." After each round, a tabulation mark would be made in the appropriate column. Something could be gained, of course, from a general class discussion concerned with reasons behind the correct order for each of the thirty sets of pictures. However, the teacher might decide instead to have more of an in-depth, diagnostic session with just those groups of photographs that all the learners arranged correctly and incorrectly. The class could probe why everyone knew the right sequence for some photos and then spend even more time on possible explanations for misinterpretations on other sets. Sound, underlying understandings tied to chronological sequence could be reinforced, and misunderstandings could be discussed and cleared up.

In later school years, the chronological arrangement of illustrative materials can become increasingly demanding and can serve many purposes. For example, if a secondary student were to be asked to order photographs of President Woodrow Wilson, taken only between 1913 and 1921 when he was in office, the learner might be deeply moved by the dreadful change in Wilson's appearance wrought by the combination of tremendous responsibilities, taxing efforts, profound disappointments, and physical and mental collapse. Photos taken of Hiroshima, Japan, before 6 August 1945, immediately after the hideous bombing; in 1950 (when permanent buildings were begun); and later—up to the present—tell their own story when studied sequentially, and they may provoke serious contemplation. A number of valuable understandings and appreciations might emerge as a budding scholar tries to determine—perhaps first by intuition and then later by independent research— the right succession of pictures of some of Frank Lloyd Wright's architectural masterpieces, such as the Solomon R. Guggenheim Museum, the Robie House, the S. C. Johnson and Son, Inc. Research Center, the Imperial Hotel, and the Kaufmann House ("Falling Water"). Meaningful aesthetic and psychological insights could be gained from working out the correct places in time of copies of paintings by Vincent van Gogh, such as *Wheat Field and Cypress Trees, The Potato Eaters, Gardening Patches on Montmartre in Winter, Armand Roulin,* and *L'Arlesienne.* A sensitive student might regard *The Potato Eaters* (1885) as heavy, dark, somber, naive, disproportionate, and even a bit clumsy, for instance, while a responsive learner could view *Wheat Field and Cypress Trees* (1889) as being vibrant, post-impressionistic, expressive, turbulent, and somewhat frightening.

Having just suggested some pictorial approaches that elementary and secondary teachers might use to make chronological sequence more meaningful, I would now like to recommend some possibilities that are more verbal and less visual.

H. Stuart Hughes has written that the "main business" of history "is narrative." He continues, "As its very name keeps recalling to our minds, history is a story. Alone of the learned disciplines, it tries to recapture how things happened." [7]

Seven- and eight-year-olds can be helped to recall events in the immediate past, to arrange these happenings in chronological order, and to write their own understandable, enjoyable history. After second and third graders have finished lunch, the teacher could ask class members to try to recall as many of that morning's activities as possible. The teacher would try to get from each girl and boy at least one forenoon incident, which could then be printed with a fairly broad liquid marker on large lined sheets of experience chart paper held on an easel in the front of the classroom. The occurrences remembered by the children probably would not appear in any special order. After all the events have been recorded, the teacher could have the children cut them apart with blunt-nosed primary scissors. Then chairs would be moved toward the walls of the classroom so the center of the floor is clear. A long piece of butcher paper would be placed on the floor. Together, the entire class would put the strips of happenings in the correct chronological sequence. The incidents could then be stapled down the length of the butcher paper, thus chronicling remembered experiences from the beginning to the end of the morning. Next, the teacher would return to the experience chart (also called "storybook") paper on the easel in the front of the room and involve everyone in the class in composing "The History of Our Morning." After the whole narrative has been printed, it can be used for especially meaningful individual reading practice, as each pupil could be invited to read the class story privately to the teacher.

Third and fourth graders, who have had experiences similar to the preceding, can be helped to write individual histories of an important class happening, such as a field trip. Following the group's return from a farm, a factory, a historical site or museum, or a children's theater production, the teacher could ask all of the participants to come one at a time to her or his desk and to whisper at least four things that happened during the excursion. The teacher would take rough notes containing 100–150 incidents reported; combine the duplications; make up a list of ten to twenty of the most significant, interesting, pleasurable, and humorous occurrences; use a typewriter with primary type to put the items on a fluid duplicator master; and run off a copy of the list for each learner. The events would be in the wrong chronological order, so each child would clip the incidents into strips, arrange the strips sequentially, and staple or paste the strips on a sheet of paper. After each class member has written a first draft of "A History of Our Trip," the teacher would read every narrative carefully; point out privately to the individual class member any errors in chronological sequence, spelling, punctuation, grammar, or syntax; have all the stories revised, written neatly, and perhaps even illustrated; and display all of the histories on the classroom walls, where they would be read and enjoyed. Next, a class committee could select the best passages from all the compositions for a composite, polished version that the teacher could type, duplicate, and send to parents and others. (It should be noted somewhere in this chapter that elementary and secondary learners need *something* worthwhile to read and to write to develop and perfect their skills, and that social studies pursuits provide an excellent vehicle for this purpose.)

From grades five through twelve, gradually more complex, abstract, varied, and substantial verbal contacts with chronological sequence could be developed and articulated by social studies teachers. At different levels and in myriad ways, learners could chronologically arrange and study developments in such diverse areas as discovery, exploration, colonization, family life, education, leisure, recreation, resources, ecology, territorial expansion, science, technology, transportation, communication, housing, immigration, population, mobility, settlement, agriculture, labor, business, industry, interest groups, social trends, law, crime, government, domestic and foreign affairs, war, peace, global interdependence, human and civil rights, the arts, ideas, and values. An eighth grade class studying the history of the United States might serve as a suitable example here. The group could be examining aspects of the era of the American Revolution from 1763 to 1789. On the classroom chalkboard, the teacher could list in incorrect chronological order some of the more easily understood events leading up to the Revolutionary War, such as the Boston Tea Party, the Boston Massacre, the Burning of the *Gaspee,* the Quartering Act, the Tea Act, the Stamp Act, and the Townshend Act. Before the arrival of the students for a class session, the teacher could arrange clusters of four or five chairs facing each other in seven different parts of the classroom. The teacher might write a number and a committee title (e.g., #1 BOSTON TEA PARTY) on each of seven 5″×8″ cards folded longitudinally down the center and could place a folded identification card on the seat of one chair in each cluster. Then, the teacher could number 3″×5″ cards from 1 to 7 until there is a card for each member of the class. As each student enters the classroom, he or she receives a numbered card, matches it with a committee number, and takes a seat in the appropriate cluster. As soon as everyone is seated, the teacher might announce that the person in each cluster with the longest last name would be the committee chairperson and that the individual in each group with the shortest last name would be the committee reporter. The classroom would be stocked well with research materials, including textbooks, encyclopedias, histories, historical novels for children and adolescents, filmstrips, and recordings. The teacher could ask every class member to gather information on his or her committee's topic. All the data would be assembled and written up by the reporter for each group. The reporters would then assemble elsewhere in the school (e.g., the library, the media center, the social studies laboratory) and would prepare a joint history of events leading up to the Revolutionary War that would place the seven incidents in proper chronological sequence and hopefully point out some interrelationships existing between and among the happenings. The teacher would check the reporters' narratives for accuracy in fact and in English and would type, reproduce, and distribute copies of the final product. After each student has read the history, a class discussion would take place. The teacher would help the class see a logic to some of the cause-and-effect relationships in the chronology. For instance, even without knowing all the dates, given events could be ordered meaningfully. It makes sense that the Tea Act of 10 May 1773 followed problems the British East India Company was having. (The company was almost bankrupt, and it had a huge surplus of tea on hand in England.) A mass meeting in Philadelphia on 16 October 1773 was in response to the Tea Act that had been passed to help save the British East India Company. A Boston town meeting on the fifth and sixth of November supported the actions taken in Philadelphia, and so on—right on up through a November 10th warning issued to New York harbor pilots against attempting to guide tea ships up the harbor, a November 29th session of the Sons of Liberty that called tea importers enemies of America and promised a boycott, and the Boston Tea Party on the sixteenth of December.[8]

A methodological procedure somewhat similar to the one just described could be used with senior high school students in American history and government and in law-related education to move learners toward an even more sophisticated understanding of chronological sequence. This time, each of six groups of five students might be clustered around related sets of cases which have come before the Supreme Court of the United States. The high school social studies teacher could get ideas for committee titles and individual, matching constitutional decisions from many books[9] in history, political science, and law readily available in college and university libraries. Based on the needs, interests, abilities, and aspirations of his or her students, the teacher could form the six class groups around general and more specific headings such as electronic surveillance, double jeopardy, the right to protest, self-incrimination, freedom of the press, the right to counsel, legislative apportionment, bail, internal security, plea-bargaining, monopoly, inciting a riot, all deliberate speed, and freedom of speech. The first time this approach is used the teacher could try these committee titles and cases: Committee #1, The Right to Equal Protection of the Laws (*Bolling v. Sharpe, Milliken v. Bradley, Dred Scott v. Sandford, Brown v. Board of Education of Topeka, Plessy v. Ferguson*); Committee #2, Unreasonable Searches and Seizures (*Olmstead v. United States, Katz v. United States, Boyd v. United States, Terry v. Ohio, Schneckloth v. Bustamonte);* Committee #3, The Right of Privacy [Freedom of Association] (*Burton v. Wilmington Parking Authority, Moose Lodge v. Irvis, Gilmore v. City of Montgomery, Shelley v. Kraemer, Daniel v. Paul*); Committee #4, Freedom of Religion (*Everson v. Board of Education, Board of Education v. Allen, Zorach v. Clauson, West Virginia State Board of Education v. Barnette, McCollum v. Board of Education*); Committee #5, Obscenity [Freedom of Expression] (*Redrup v. New York, Roth v. United States, A Book Named "John Cleland's Memoirs of a Woman of Pleasure"* ["Fanny Hill"] *v. Attorney General of Massachusetts, Butler v. Michigan, Ginzburg v. United States*); and Committee #6, The Death Penalty (*Gregg v. Georgia, McGautha v. California, Turman v. Georgia, Witherspoon v. Illinois, Woodson v. North Carolina*). [For instructional purposes here, the preceding cases have been arranged carefully in incorrect chronological order, and the dates of decisions have been deliberately omitted. During the beginning stages of this procedure, the teacher could use this erroneous sequence, should he or she have occasion to list the cases on the chalkboard, in class handouts, etc.] The teacher could prepare a simple, direct, readable digest of the background for each case, key developments, the basics of opinions delivered, and a summary of what the Court held. All dates and references to previous cases would be omitted. Then, each committee member would present his or her case to the other four students. Following a good, solid discussion—during which the teacher might move from group to group to answer questions briefly— each cluster would attempt to figure out the chronological sequence of its five cases.

Members of Committee #1 might remember something about *Dred Scott* v. *Sandford, Plessy* v. *Ferguson,* and *Brown* v. *Board of Education of Topeka* from previous study, or it could think through that sequence with the information the teacher has provided. The majority of the Court held that Dred Scott was not a citizen of the United States or of the state of Missouri, and, thus, that he could not sue in the federal courts. In *Plessy* v. *Ferguson,* Mr. Justice Brown, a northerner, pointed out that the Court had frequently drawn a distinction between laws interfering with the political equality of the Negro and those requiring the separation of the two races in schools, theaters, and railway carriages, and he enunciated the "separate but equal" formula for the majority. Mr. Justice Harlan, a southerner, wrote a strong dissenting opinion, denying "that any legislative body or judicial tribunal may have regard to the race of citizens when the civil rights of those citizens are involved."[10] For a unanimous bench in *Brown* v. *Board of Education of Topeka* (1954), Mr. Chief Justice Warren delivered the opinion that "in the field of public education the doctrine of 'separate but equal' has no place. Separate educational facilities are inherently unequal."[11] Although students in Committee #1 might not recall *Bolling* v. *Sharpe* (1954), which challenged the validity of segregation in public schools of the District of Columbia, the teacher might include in his or her digest of the case some helpful portions of Mr. Chief Justice Warren's opinion. The Chief Justice wrote:

> We have *this day* [italics mine] held that the Equal Protection Clause of the Fourteenth Amendment prohibits the states from maintaining racially segregated public schools....
>
> In view of our decision that the Constitution prohibits the states from maintaining racially segregated public schools, it would be unthinkable that the same Constitution would impose a lesser duty on the Federal Government....[12]

In *Milliken* v. *Bradley* (1974), the Supreme Court rejected by a 5-4 vote a multi-district remedy for a segregation problem in a single school district. A portion of the dissenting opinion—by Mr. Justice Marshall, who was joined by Mr. Justice Douglas, Mr. Justice Brennan, and Mr. Justice White—appears below and offers a nice clue for chronological placement. This quotation could also launch an excellent committee (and later even a complete class) discussion, for the sensitive case might introduce the question of whether Supreme Court decisions are always increasingly "intelligent," "humane," "fair," "liberal," or whatever other words might be used, or whether members of the Court are human beings who sometimes err, contradict themselves, respond to pressures of the times, become senile, and so on. In any event, here is part of the dissenting opinion:

> In [a previous case], ... this Court held that segregation of children in public schools on the basis of race deprives minority group children of equal educational opportunities and therefore denies them the equal protection of the laws under the Fourteenth Amendment. ... [T]his Court has not been diverted from its appointed task of making "a living truth" of our constitutional idea of equal justice under law. ...
> After 20 years of small, often difficult steps toward that great end, the Court today takes a giant step backwards. ...[13]

After each of the six committees has decided on what it believes to be the correct chronological sequence of its five cases, the actual dates of decisions would be looked up and entered on the teacher's digests of the thirty cases. Any errors in chronological arrangement would be corrected at this point. This would be a good time for the teacher to help the entire class focus on the concept of legal precedence and its close relationship to chronological sequence. Using sources such as those listed in note 9, the teacher could read aloud to the class from those parts of the most recent cases that refer to the previous relevant decisions in chronological order. Finally, on the chalkboard or on a time line on a long strip of butcher paper, the teacher might list chronologically all of the thirty cases (including the dates) used by the whole class. The teacher might then ask class members whether they can discern any possible trends, patterns, consistencies, or inconsistencies around the same time and over the years between and among cases in the six classifications used for committee titles.

The last suggestion in this chapter that is designed to make chronological sequence meaningful should appeal to learners from nine to ninety. It might be visual and/or verbal, and it could be very simple or really complex. It centers on genealogy, and it offers a slightly different twist to chronology and seems to be more fun if it is approached "backward" from the present to the past, from a student to his or her forebears. Genealogical activities in elementary and secondary schools are especially successful and gratifying if children and youth are motivated well, given some preparation by the teacher or time to prepare themselves, allowed to carry out certain of their projects over a period of weeks along with other daily social studies activities, and encouraged to talk and work with family members close at hand and to correspond with relatives farther away. Of course, a field trip to an appropriate library, archive, or genealogical society could facilitate independent research considerably, especially if interested, willing, and available parents and other adult helpers are included.

Alex Haley's genealogical novel *Roots* has attracted a tremendous amount of attention and has greatly stimulated interest in family history. An estimated 130 million Americans watched the eight-part television version of *Roots* in January 1977. At different grade levels, the teacher might launch various genealogical activities by reading from *Roots* to younger students, asking older students to read all or part of it, and/or playing portions of the record *Alex Haley Tells the Story of His Search for Roots*.[14] Next, with learners in the fourth through the sixth grades and with less able readers in higher grades, the teacher might read from books [15] on genealogy. Most older students, of course, could read similar sources themselves. A number of these books on genealogy are clear, simple, and interesting, and they can be very helpful.

Having worked out a way to copy photographs for the chronological sequence exercise illustrated in figure 2, the fourth through twelfth grade teacher might use a visual approach to genealogy which could involve and please many learners and their families. The idea is to have class members bring photographs of themselves, their parents, their grandparents, and their great-grandparents, if possible; to copy the photographs in different ways and sizes; and to inspire each learner who can and wants to participate in this activity to create some kind of a visual which can be displayed first in the classroom and then taken home for the family to enjoy and even cherish. The generations might be arranged on a flat surface or in three dimensions in the form of a family tree, a triangle, a pyramid, a stack of blocks, a ziggurat, or a mobile. Figure 3 illustrates some possibilities. Or, the names of relatives could be

Figure 3.

Figure 3 *(Continued)*

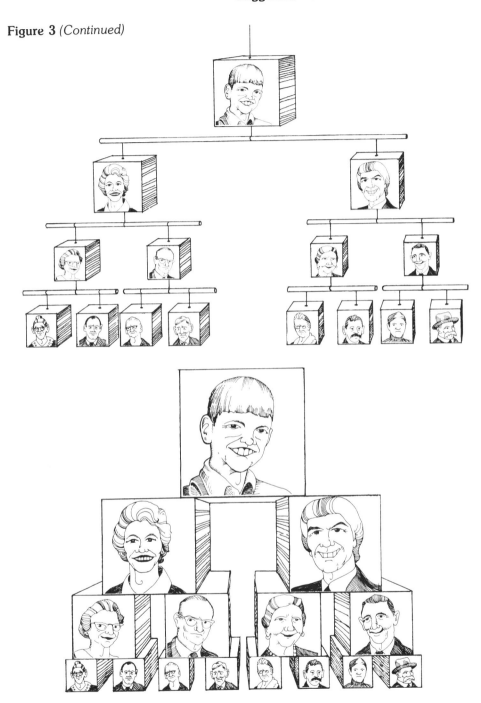

lettered and displayed in some visual form, such as a genealogical fan or four-generation pedigree chart, as shown in figure 4. Tombstone rubbings suggest yet another medium by which elementary and secondary learners might portray their lineage. In parts of New England, rural America, and other areas, grave markers can help children and youth recall their progenitors' arrivals and departures, joys and sorrows. In the Wheatland Presbyterian Church Cemetery in Breda, Iowa, for example, one of my sons would be able to do rubbings of inscriptions on his mother's side of the family all the way back to his great-great-grandparents. If pupils do not have relatives in the community where they now live, they might trace the chronology of a well-established family, buried for generations in an old cemetery. The teacher could show students how to stretch rice paper tightly on a tombstone with masking tape so an Oldstone rubbing stone crayon or an engineering crayon can be used to get a nice image of the inscription. Rubbings prepared by class members could be displayed on the hallway walls of a school so many pupils and others could see them. The teacher might do a few rubbings to add interest to the project, such as my favorite inscription: "I told them I was sick!"

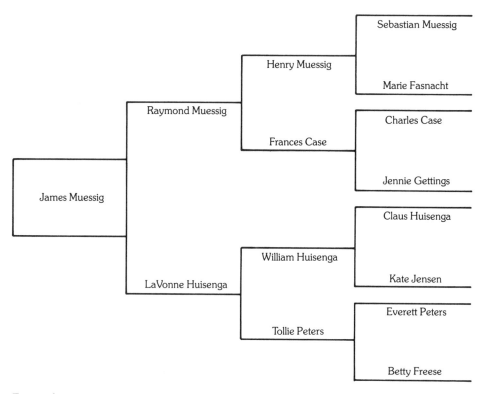

Figure 4.

With respect to chronological sequence in general and genealogy in particular, my final suggestion in this chapter for elementary and secondary teachers is to encourage each learner from the sixth through the twelfth grades to give an oral report on a genealogical subject of interest to him or her. The three imaginary oral reports which follow have been created to illustrate some of the possibilities in this activity. If a class member cannot secure or share information on his or her family history for various reasons, he or she can get practice with "reverse" chronology by investigating the pedigree of an animal or the lineage of a famous person, as the first two examples below demonstrate.

I'm really into horses, like a lot of girls my age. OK? So I had fun finding out about the bloodlines of a thoroughbred race horse named Nijinsky. Well, I really did only one bloodline, 'cause there were thirty-two horses when I got back five generations! Anyway—and I hope I get the words right—, Nijinsky's father—called a sire, I think— was Northern Dancer. The mother—a dam—was Flaming Page. I'll stick with the family of Flaming Page now. She was the foal of Bull Page and Flaring Top. Nijinsky's great-grandsires on the dam side were Bull Lea and Menow. The great-grandams were Our Page and Flaming Top. Bull Lea was out of Bull Dog and Rose Leaves. Don't horses have interesting names sometimes?! Our Page was from Blue Larkspur and Occult. Menow was the foal of Pharamond and Alcibiades. Flaming Top had Omaha for a sire and Firetop for a dam. But it gets really good five generations back. In the list of great-great-great-grandsires are two of the most famous thoroughbred horses in the whole history of racing, Gallant Fox and Man o' War. Now, there's a pedigree chart![16] *I stay with my grandma, and she told me that there are people in racing that know the bloodlines of quite a few important thoroughbreds all the way back five generations, and that a lot of owners of thoroughbreds can tell you the pedigrees of their horses back at least three generations. I mean, genealogy is really important when it comes to expensive horses. Maybe that's true of registered cattle, and purebred dogs, and cats that are shown, and stuff.*

* * *

Two of my best friends are in this class, and they know that I moved in just a few months ago with new foster parents. I don't know anything about my natural parents. Even though we didn't have to do some kind of genealogy project for this class if we didn't want to, I didn't want to be left out. So, I decided to pick somebody famous. I started with President Franklin Delano Roosevelt, but that looked like it was going to be too hard. He was related by blood or through marriage to eleven former Presidents. They were Washington, John Adams, Madison, John Quincy Adams, Van Buren, William Henry Harrison, Taylor, Grant, Benjamin Harrison, Theodore Roosevelt, and Taft.[17] *Franklin Roosevelt's ancestry was really mixed and went back to seven or eight countries, it looks like. He even married a distant cousin, Anna Eleanor Roosevelt. Eleanor's uncle was Theodore Roosevelt. He gave her away at the wedding. Theodore Roosevelt and Franklin were fifth cousins. Well, you can see why I gave up on this and then chose Abraham Lincoln—who was easier, but interesting, anyway.*

I'll go backward in time. Abraham Lincoln's mother was Nancy Hanks. Her mother was Lucy Hanks. There isn't much known about the Hanks family. There isn't anything in the records about the father of Nancy Hanks.

Abraham Lincoln's father was Thomas Lincoln, and his grandfather was Abraham Lincoln. The grandfather was a captain of the Virginia militia during the Revolutionary War. His family moved to Kentucky in 1782. He was killed by an Indian.

Let's see ... John Lincoln was the father of President Lincoln's grandfather. I think Mordecai Lincoln was John Lincoln's grandfather. Anyway, the American branch of President Lincoln's family goes back to Samuel Lincoln, Mordecai's father. Samuel Lincoln was a weaver. He came from England to Massachusetts in 1637. Pretty good, huh?

That's as far as I got. But I'll bet you could find out a lot more in England. If I figured it out right, there is a city of Lincoln in a big county of Lincoln that has three Lincolnshires in it. The "Earls of Lincoln" is an English title that was created abound 1139. There is a Lincoln castle that was founded by William the Conqueror, and there is a Lincoln cathedral that is really old too. But I don't know, really, if any of this connects with the sixteenth president. It could be that the Lincolns at least got the family name from that part of England.

* * *

To be honest, I wasn't really turned on by this project at first. I like sports a lot. But when I told my dad about it, he said it was a "super idea." He's been interested in genealogy for years, but he's never had enough free time to get serious about it. He told me that he had the best information so far on my Great-Grandfather Case's side of the family. Dad hauled out his baby book, an old family Bible, and a copy he had bought of David O'Killia the Immigrant of Old Yarmouth, Massachusetts with His Descendants and Allied Families: 1652-1962.[18] *My Great-Aunt Lucy Case lives with us—she's 97, would you believe—, and she had some notes she had taken over the years and a helpful little book called* Old Home Week Celebration in Centerville, Massachusetts, August 19—22, 1904: Historical Notes.[19] *I'm not all that sure about the stuff I'm going to tell you now; but I'm going to check it out—because I've become interested—with a great-great-step-cousin-by-marriage, Alice Case, in Wiscasset, Maine, who is a real genealogist.*

My great-grandfather was Charles Phinney Case, a son of John Cahoon Case and Lydia Phinney. John was the captain of the Emma Bacon, *from which he was lost overboard in 1869. Lot Case and Eliza Cahoon were the parents of John C. Case. Lot Case was the son of Ebenezer Case and Martha Lewis. Ebenezer fought in the American Revolutionary War, and we have his powder horn in our home. Isaac Case and Martha Phinney were Ebenezer's mother and father. Isaac was one of the six children of Ebenezer Case and Elizabeth Lewis, whose names appear on an "intention" published on July 2, 1726. This Ebenezer was the son of William Case and Hope Hamlin. In one set of Aunt Lucy's notes, it says that Hope Hamlin was a Mayflower descendant, no less! But I don't have any real proof yet. Then, if I have it right, the father of William was the earliest of the Ebenezers in the American Case line, who came to Roxbury, Massachusetts sometime before 1690 and who married Patience Draper. I can't make any earlier connections, but there was a Johanne Case of Yorkshire about 1379, a Stephen Casse of Somertshire around 1327, and a Casse Rumpe of County Kent, England in 1275. Maybe they were early relatives.*

Oh, just one other thing before I sit down. My Great-Grandmother Case was Jennie Gettings, a descendant of "The Great O'Gara of Coolavin" in Ireland. An Oliver O'Gara sat in the Dublin Parliament in 1689 for County Sligo. A little over 100 miles from Dublin, around 5,000 years ago, there was a Stone Age city on the lake bed of Lough Gara in County Sligo. That may be where the Irish side of my family started. How's that for roots?!

Inviting Learners to Become Historical Detectives

In *The Historian as Detective: Essays on Evidence,* Robin W. Winks observes, "The historian must collect, interpret, and then explain his evidence by methods which are not greatly different from those techniques employed by the detective, or at least the detective of fiction."[20] Winks adds that daily, in small ways, all of us are detectives and historians, "in that we reconstruct past events from present evidence, and perhaps we build usable generalizations upon those reconstructions."[21] Although Sir Arthur Conan Doyle has been credited with being the father of scientific criminology, the patron saint of the detective story, and the creator of "the most famous character in the English language,"[22] Doyle must also accept some of the blame for the confusion that often exists between *deduction* (the word Doyle used incorrectly so frequently, which really means moving from the general to the particular) and *induction* (proceeding from the particular to the general, as Sherlock Holmes so often did in his memorable cases). When we social studies teachers help elementary and secondary learners to gather pieces of the past (isolated names, dates, places, facts, happenings, etc.) and to assemble these parts into meaningful wholes (generalizations, which interrelate two or more concepts), we are guiding *inductive* reasoning. When we assist children and youth to begin with significant historical generalizations and then to identify specific instances in the past which match those generalizations, we are fostering *deductive* behavior. Of course, in complex thought processes, such as the reflective examination of a controversial issue, one can move back and forth between the particular and the general as necessary.

For his useful and enjoyable book, Winks has chosen cases carefully "in order to point up the element of evidence within them, to emphasize leads and clues, straight tips and false rumors, and the mischief wrought by time..." with the thought that the essays "represent a close fictional parallel to the historical problem under discussion ...."[23] The teacher's reading of *The Historian as Detective* might inspire a number of methodological approaches in addition to the ideas I have developed for this portion of the chapter.

Fritz Stern has written in *The Varieties of History* that some historians "delight in tracking down an elusive source, in finding, often accidentally, a clue to some obscure problem, others in trying to infer the meaning of an event, the spirit of an age, the causes of a crisis."[24] In either case, the *delight* is there, and the enjoyment of younger and older learners has been an important consideration in the suggestions which now follow.

From the intermediate grades on through the senior high school, the teacher could initiate the process of inviting learners to become historical detectives by having groups of three to six class members play the "Clue"[25] detective game manufactured by Parker Brothers. A few days in advance of this motivational activity, designed to get pupils into a "Who-done-it?" spirit, the teacher would indicate that five to ten sets of "Clue" will be needed. Students could bring their own games and/or borrow them from friends. Perhaps forty to fifty minutes, or a whole period, could be allocated for playing the game one day, with a follow-up discussion anticipated the next day. In order to solve the murder of Mr. Boddy in his mansion, participants must find out *who* among six suspects (Col. Mustard, etc.) committed the crime, *where* among six places (the study, etc.) the act took place, and *how* among six possible weapons (a candlestick, etc.) the dreadful deed was perpetrated. As stated in the rules, "The player who, by the process of deduction [sic] and good plain common sense, first identifies the 3 solution cards hidden in the little envelope, wins the game." Winners could be interviewed by the teacher as a part of the follow-up session to see if some kind of "system" had been tried and found successful. For enrichment purposes with secondary students, a mathematics teacher might be invited to the social studies class to explain the relationship of probability to the "Clue" game ($6 \times 6 \times 6 = 216$, etc.).

After the class discussion of the "Clue" game, the teacher might move elementary and secondary learners into detective short stories and novels. To give children and youth a feeling for the appeal of the genre of mystery literature, the teacher could begin by reading aloud to the total group something brief and intriguing. At the intermediate grade level, for example, the teacher might select "The Case of the Two-Dollar Bill," [26] an easily read and understood story of less than 1,000 words, involving ten-year-old Encyclopedia Brown, a police chief's only child, who is proclaimed on the back cover of a collection of his adventures as "famous for his powers of crime detection and America's favorite super-sleuth." Each Encyclopedia case provides clues to the attentive younger listener (and later reader, hopefully), concludes with a mystery to be solved, and then has an accompanying, one-page solution in the back of the book. The junior high school social studies teacher might read aloud to his or her class John D. MacDonald's short story "The Homesick Buick." [27] Students in grades seven through nine are almost sure to enjoy this account, for it is fast-paced, funny, and very readable, and its hero is a delightful fourteen-year-old, Pink Dee. The Buick in the title is the only clue in a daring bank robbery. The police are stumped. Pink uses the push-button settings on the car radio to figure out the possible location of the robbers' hideout, and the criminals are nabbed. With respect to the teaching of history, per se, MacDonald's story offers some nice possibilities. For example, the following paragraph might spark a discussion on eyewitness accounts in history:

> No one had taken down a single license number. But it was positively established that the other two cars had been either two- or four-door sedans in dark blue, black, green, or maroon, and that they had been either Buicks, Nashes, Oldsmobiles, Chryslers, Pontiacs or Packards—or maybe Hudsons. And one lone woman held out for convertible Cadillacs. For each person that insisted that they had Mississippi registration, there was one equally insistent on Louisiana, Texas, Alabama, New Mexico, and Oklahoma. And one old lady said that she guessed she knew a California plate when she saw one. [28]

There are innumerable fine detective short stories, of course, which the senior high school teacher might read aloud, such as Georges Simenon's "Mme. Maigret's Admirer." [29] However, I recommend a very brief, "classic" passage in Chapter 1, "The Science of Deduction," found in *The Sign of Four* by Sir Arthur Conan Doyle. [30] The teacher could start with Dr. Watson saying, "I have heard you say it is

Figure 5-A.

Figure 5-B.

difficult for a man . . . '' and end with Holmes asking, "Where is the mystery in all this?" Beginning with a watch recently received by Watson, Holmes finds one clue after another, in good detective fashion, until he arrives inductively at a generalization regarding the former owner of the timepiece.

At this point in a series of approaches designed to help elementary and secondary learners become historical detectives, the teacher might ask each class member to read at least one suspense novel. "Who-done-it?" books motivate learners to read for they are readily available in inexpensive paperbacks, written from the fourth grade on through to the adult reading level, likely to stimulate readers to think and to keep interested, and quite often created by good authors, such as G. K. Chesterton, Agatha Christie, Dashiell Hammett, John D. MacDonald, Ellery Queen, Dorothy L. Sayers, and Josephine Tey. For each grade-level range—intermediate, junior high, and senior high—there are detective novels[31] available.

Now, budding historical detectives should be ready to develop their inductive reasoning powers by working with historical "Whatsits?" and/or realia. The teacher might begin this exercise with one "Whatsit?," such as the object pictured in figures 5-A and 5-B. The class would be gathered closely around the teacher. The teacher would ask everyone to be perfectly quiet and would explain that there would be no questions or comments at this time. The object would be held at different heights and angles and rotated slowly. In this instance, the two pieces of wood would be raised and lowered, as they have been in figures 5-A and 5-B. Next, each learner would be given a 3″×5″ card, asked to guess what the "Whatsit?" is, invited to write his or her guess on the card, and requested to turn in the card. The teacher would then read aloud to the class all of the guesses to see if anyone guessed that this "Whatsit?" is a rat trap. The next day, each class member would have his or her own real "Whatsit?" or photograph of an object from the past, as illustrated in figure 6. (The reader is encouraged now to look at the pictures in figure 6 and to guess what each "Whatsit?" is. Note 32 at the end of the chapter identifies each object.) Every pupil would be given time to study his or her "Whatsit?" carefully, to take notes on details observed on the object, and to assemble the notes into a paragraph culminating in a guess regarding what the item is. The teacher would read the paragraphs and guesses, point out key clues that may have been overlooked, and offer suggestions on ways students could sharpen their powers of observation. Class members might exchange the "Whatsits?" another time or two to gain further practice in going inductively from particulars observed to a general guess based on the observations. Then, the teacher could plan a more difficult and challenging assignment around realia that can tell an interesting story after initial examination and further investigation, such as old coins, stamps, medals, badges, uniform buttons, helmets, hats, garments, toys, license plates, books, marriage certificates, naturalization papers, commemorative plates, and daguerreotypes. The teacher would use his or her own imagination and would request the help of relatives, friends, fellow teachers, and class members in assembling enough choice objects for everyone in class. Items might be found by rummaging through basements, garages, attics, or cedar chests. (The search might be half the fun!) In the examples illustrated in figure 7, 7-A and 7-B show both sides of the *Lusitania* medal which will be discussed shortly. Figure 7-C is an 1892 American half dollar which commemorates the World's Columbian Exposition held in Chicago in 1893, when electricity was the exposition's greatest wonder and Thomas A. Edison's phonograph and Pullman cars were displayed. In scrimshaw, on the whale's tooth

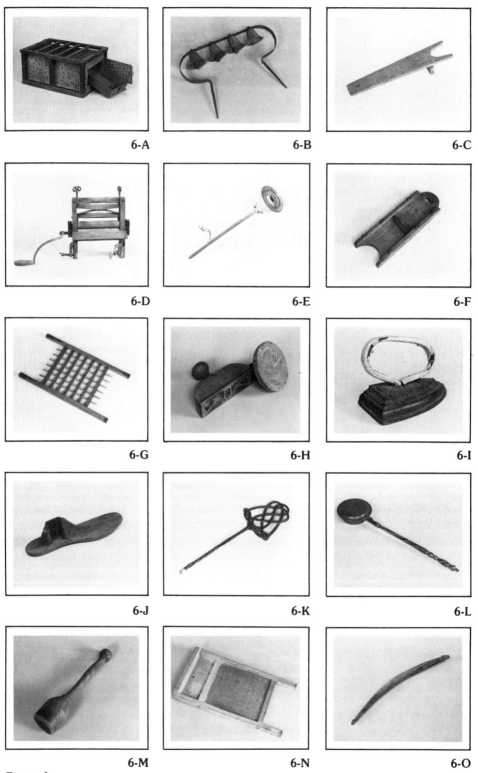

6-A   6-B   6-C

6-D   6-E   6-F

6-G   6-H   6-I

6-J   6-K   6-L

6-M   6-N   6-O

Figure 6.

seen in figure 7-D, a student could see the picture of a whale and read, "Old Whaling Port, New Bedford MASS." The engraved, gold, Elgin pocket watch photographed for figure 7-E was made in 1894 and is still being used. Figure 7-F is the title page of an early editon of Harriet Beecher Stowe's *Uncle Tom's Cabin or Life Among the Lowly,* a book with a story, indeed. The powder horn in figure 7-G was carried during the American Revolutionary War. The jubilee medal in figure 7-H was issued in 1898 when there was still a Saxony. (The state of Saxony was abolished as a political unit by the East German government in 1952.) Each student could bring and research his or her own object. Or, a learner might make a selection from the class pool of intriguing realia. Or, based on known interests and demonstrated abilities of class members, the insightful teacher could suggest something appropriate for a given pupil. From each "historical detective," the teacher might request a written "detective report" in two parts. The first part might be entitled, simply, "What I Saw First" and would concern details observed during the initial examination of the object. It would be written in the present tense as clues are acquired. The second phase could be called "What I Found Out Later" and would deal with information gained through reading, talking with others, and so on. A make-believe example follows.

DETECTIVE REPORT

The *Lusitania* Medal

by

Reelee Eegre, Historical Detective

Part I: What I Saw First
I see a round piece of metal. [Figure 7-A] It has a dull color. It may be a coin or a medal. On one side, there is a skeleton—selling tickets to a movie or a Halloween program, maybe. There is lettering next to the ticket booth, but I can't make it out very well. I see "UNARD" and "CUN" and "LINI," or something. There are a lot of people crowding to buy tickets. One man is reading a newspaper with light lettering on it that I can't figure out. Way up on top I see more lettering that looks like "GESCHAFTVBERALLES." This must be something foreign.
On the other side of the coin or medal [Figure 7-B], there is a boat in the water, The boat seems to have a lot of stuff on top of the deck. Could there be a cannon there or something? Is the boat sinking? On the top are letters again. They look like "EINE BANN WARE" to me. Then, there are more letters on the bottom, like "LVSITANIA" and "5 MAY 1915" and other things. I think "DER" and "EIN" might be German words. Maybe the "V" is supposed to be a "U" in some of the words. That one kind of bigger word by itself might be "LUSITANIA," which was a ship that was sunk sometime. Was it 1915, like the date says?

Part II: What I Found Out Later
In our school library, the librarian helped me find a German-American dictionary. I started to pick out each word I could make out on the coin, but that was slow going. The library also had a shelf of American history textbooks, collected over the years. I looked under Lusitania *in the index of two newer*

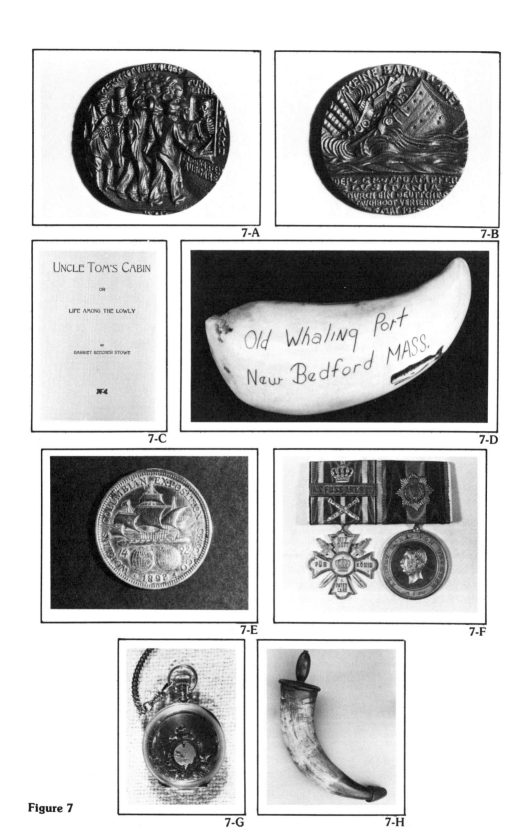

7-A

7-B

7-C

7-D

7-E

7-F

Figure 7

7-G

7-H

110

ones. One didn't have anything, and the other only had a sentence or two. Then, I found an older textbook that said that the Lusitania *was an English Cunard passenger liner. Some of those letters on the medal must be parts of "CUNARD." The ship was hit by two or three German submarine torpedoes on 7 May 1915. So, the words could be German. The month and year seem to check out, but not the day. Almost 2,000 people were aboard the helpless ship. About 1,000 died. That included 124 Americans. The tragedy helped get the United States into World War I, according to the older textbook. But I didn't find anything about the coin. I looked in the card catalog in the school library for a book just on the* Lusitania, *but there wasn't one. I located a book on ships that had the* Lusitania *in it, but it was about the size and speed and stuff, not the medal.*

That night, my dad said he was headed for a photography store in a big shopping center. I asked him to please do me a favor and to see if the paperback bookstore in the shopping center might have something inexpensive on the Lusitania. *Dad likes books and me, and he brought home two books,* The Last Voyage of the Lusitania *by Hoehling and Hoehling* [33] *and* The Lusitania *by Simpson.* [34] *I struck oil! Both books had something about the* Lusitania *medal! And Simpson even has pictures of both sides of the very same medal I was investigating, with a caption that says, "The British propaganda replica of the German medal originally struck to satirize the sailing of the* Lusitania *rather than to celebrate her sinking."* [35] *Then, I asked a neighbor who has been in the U.S. Army in Germany recently to help me with the printing. So, using the two books Dad got and the neighbor's help, I'll try to put it all together quickly.*

A German by the name of Goetz designed the medal and made about forty copies of it for a joke. He wanted to show in a sort of kidding way that the Lusitania *was carrying illegal cargoes, like war things. The things I couldn't make out on the deck of the ship shown in the medal are supposed to a cannon, a tank, and an airplane, and like that. My neighbor thinks that "Keine Bannware" means "no contraband." Death is selling tickets, and the booth has to do with the Cunard Lines company that owned the ship. When Goetz put "Geschaft uber alles," on the medal, he meant that Cunard was putting "business over all," risking the lives of passengers by carrying contraband.*

But now the story gets kinda nasty. According to Simpson's book—that I thought was really complete and a lot of help — a department store owner in England made 300,000 copies of the Goetz medal. The English copies were sent all over the world to make people hate Germany, and maybe worked as propaganda. [36] *As near as I can figure it out, people were supposed to get the idea that the Germans had made the medal to brag about sinking the ship and killing all of those helpless people.*

Well, I can quit there, I guess, as far as the medal goes. But I want to throw in some other things I learned from reading the two books on the Lusitania. *A lot of Americans and others must have been really informed wrong and even lied to on the* Lusitania *thing. I wonder how many people ever did get later facts like some I'm going to tell now.*

Long before the sinking, the Lusitania *had secretly been turned into an armed auxiliary cruiser. Her six-inch guns didn't make her a battleship, but she could sure sink a submarine. She had orders to ram any sub on sight. Most of her cargo was contraband and included almost 5,000 boxes of cartridges, cases of shrap-nel shells, maybe even stuff for poison gas. There were Canadian troops on board too. The Germans put ads in newspapers to warn people not to sail on the ship. A German told the American Secretary of State all about the illegal cargo and how America wasn't behaving like a neutral country. Only one torpedo was fired by the sub, and it probably would not have sunk the* Lusitania. *The boilers didn't explode from the hit, but the stuff on board sure did. There had not been lifeboat drills. A lot of the crew was inexperienced. The ship was not protected. A British cruiser that was supposed to meet and help the* Lusitania *was called back. The whole thing was a mess! Even President Woodrow Wilson tried to cover up the real facts. It is some story.*

Do I get extra credit for all of this work?

Detective Eegre

After all of the detective reports on compelling realia have been received and critiqued by the teacher, and corrected and copied neatly by all members of the class, the teacher might plan an early evening, open house event in the school cafeteria, gymnasium, or some other large room. Parents, friends of the teacher, and others could be asked to attend and to bring refreshments. Each pupil would be seated at a desk or a small table with his or her object and detective report and would be prepared to tell parents and others about the item and to answer questions. The best kind of museum for children and youth is a teaching museum, not just a repository. And the class would have created its own miniature teaching museum for one night!

This next methodological suggestion for emerging historical detectives in grades four through twelve has many appealing features. It can be started easily by a beginning teacher, and it can be perfected over a period of years by an experienced classroom artist. Unlike lesson plans and resource units, which require blocks of time for organization and writing, the idea being set forth here can be carried out a piece at a time, whenever the teacher has a few "spare" minutes. This approach can be adapted for use with local, state, regional, American, and world history, for the humanities, for multiethnic and women's studies, and so forth. Its components can range from easy to difficult, humorous to serious, and the like. This recommendation can be tailored to less able and reluctant readers, pupils with short attention spans, individuals who "get done early" and become behavior problems, gifted children and youth who need and want enrichment in and out of the classroom, and so on. It can introduce and reinforce varied understandings, skills, appreciations, and values. It can progress from a small kitchen recipe box for 3"×5" cards to a long drawer.

But a word of warning may be appropriate at this point. Most of the information likely to be secured by developing historical detectives in this context is trivial in and of itself. It is the investigation, the search, the process, rather, that is important. Girls and boys, young women and young men, need to learn how and where to locate data, and that is what we are after here, not to mention some occasional fun.

Very simply, the teacher has 3"×5" cards close at hand in the classroom, at home, etc., and uses his or her memory, textbooks, specific histories and biographies, books of facts, sets of encyclopedias, or other sources to come up with single questions and short series of related questions to write on the cards. The teacher might award extra credit points according to the difficulty level of each question card. If a recipe box is used at first, alphabetical dividers or index cards for "Biscuits-Bread," "Cakes," etc., could be covered with masking tape on which "5 POINTS," "8 POINTS," etc., would be lettered. A student would pick the difficulty level himself or herself and would select from a number of cards behind a point divider the most appealing question. Below are some examples of possible items, just to gives the teacher a feeling for possibilities inherent in the individual detective questions. (The answers come at no extra charge.)

What caused the death of Meriwether Lewis? (It is still a mystery whether his death resulted from murder or suicide.)

Where is the final resting place of Amelia Earhart (Putnam), the famous American aviation pioneer? (Her plane disappeared somewhere around Howland Island in the South Pacific on July 2, 1937, when she was attempting a round-the-world flight. She was never found.)

What was the name of Robert E. Lee's beloved horse? (Traveler.)

What was the estimated total population of the United States in 1790? (Just under four million.)

Who was the first American to receive the Nobel Prize? (Theodore Roosevelt.)

What "trick" did Napoleon I play at his coronation ceremony? (Pope Pius VII was supposed to place the crown on the Emperor's head, but the "Little Corporal" took the crown from the pontiff and placed it on his own head.)

Who was the first black to attend an inaugural reception at the White House and to be greeted by the President of the United States? (Frederick Douglass, whom Abraham Lincoln welcomed as a friend.)

What is unusual about the burial of Ben Jonson, the famous English dramatist and poet, in Westminster Abbey? (In accordance with his instructions, he was buried standing up.)

Who was the first President of the United States to ride on a railroad train powered by a diesel locomotive? (Franklin Delano Roosevelt.)

What was the pseudonym adopted by Amandine Aurore Lucile Dupin Dudevant in 1832? (George Sand.)

Who is buried in Grant's Tomb on Riverside Drive in New York City? (This may not be as easy as it seems, for Ulysses S. Grant *and* Julia Dent Grant, his wife, are *both* buried in the memorial tomb.)

Did King John of England sign the Magna Carta in 1215? (No, he *sealed* it. It is doubtful whether King John could write.)

In 1868, with the help of some friends, Susan Brownell Anthony started a publication concerned with the rights of women. What was the title of this magazine? (*The Revolution.*)

What was the "strange" dessert Dorothy (Dolley) Madison served to guests at a White House dinner in 1809? (Ice cream.)

How did Portland, Oregon get its name? (A toss of a coin in 1845 decided Portland's name. Francis W. Pettygrove and Amos W. Lovejoy, two early settlers, preferred the names of Portland and Boston, respectively. They chose the coin toss as a way of deciding, and Pettygrove won.)

How did French taxicabs help to stop the advance of the Germans at the Battle of the Marne during World War I? (General Joseph Gallieni, the military governor of Paris, used hundreds of taxis to carry thousands of soldiers in a very short time from Paris to the Marne, thus checking the attack at a critical time.)

Who was the first President of the United States to wear a beard? (Abraham Lincoln.)

Jim Thorpe was one of the greatest all-round athletes of all time and was outstanding in the 1912 Olympic Games at Stockholm. Why, then, were his gold medals and trophy later taken from him and his Olympic records removed from the books? (It was discovered that he had played semiprofessional baseball in the summer of 1911.)

How long did it take to build the Cologne Cathedral? (632 years. The project was started in 1248 and completed in 1880.)

In 1454, Johann Gutenberg completed the first Bible ever printed. The project took two years, for each character and symbol had to be fashioned by hand. How many pieces were there in all? (46,000.)

From what source did Lorraine Hansberry get the inspiration for the title of her play *A Raisin in the Sun?* (A poem by Langston Hughes.)

How many automobiles were registered in the U. S. in 1900? (8,000.)

Edith Louisa Cavell was a British nurse, a humanitarian, and a World War I martyr. She was shot by the Germans in Brussels on October 12, 1915. What were her last words? ("I realize that patriotism is not enough. I must have no hatred or bitterness towards anyone.")

Babylon was a magnificent ancient city and the capital of Babylonia. What does the word "Babylon" mean? ("Gate of the god.")

Has a political party ever nominated a woman as a candidate for President of the United States? (Yes. In 1872, the Equal Rights Party chose Victoria Claflin Woodhull.)

This is a three-part historical detective assignment in which you are challenged to uncover the answers to these questions: (1) How is it possible to see the horse of Napoleon I when the "Little Corporal" died over one-hundred-fifty years ago? (The horse was preserved by a taxidermist and is on display at the Place des Invalides in Paris.) (2) What is the horse's name? (Vizir.) (3) What does the name of the horse mean? (A "vizir" or "vizier" was a "high official," especially a "minister of state," in some Muslim countries and caliphates. There is a Turkish meaning, too, having to do with "carrying a burden," which would have been appropriate.)

At this point, unfolding historical detectives should be ready to investigate more substantial cases in history. They might look into yet unsolved mysteries in history to see what is known and what still baffles researchers. They could check out some widely accepted reports, beliefs, myths, both past and present, to see how well they were and are supported by the available historical evidence. The idea here is not to try to produce skeptics, debunkers, cynics, and iconoclasts, but rather to encourage learners to check out facts as a part of the larger reflective process of warranting their beliefs. Josh Billings (Henry Wheeler Shaw), the American humorist, captured part of the spirit of the idea when he said, "It ain't what a man don't know that makes him a fool, but what he does know that ain't so." And so did Carl Becker, who wrote that we should admit that there are two histories: the actual series of events that once occurred; and the ideal series that we affirm and hold in memory. The first is absolute and unchanged—it was what it was whatever we do or say about it; the second is relative, always changing in response to the increase or refinement of knowledge. . . . [37]

Although *The Historian's Craft* by Marc Bloch was written in 1941, much of it is still timely and forceful. He wrote, "It is a scandal that in our age, which is more than ever exposed to the poisons of fraud and false rumor, the critical method is so completely absent from our school programs." [38] And, Louis Gottschalk, too, got at a facet of this whole area in the following passage from *Understanding History: A Primer of Historical Method:*

> . . . Yet even in adolescent education, when the truth can be determined by historical methods, perhaps it should be presented unvarnished. A patriotism which rests on historical legends cannot be a lasting patriotism. No patriot serves his country well who hides the clay feet of his country's idols beneath layers of gilt. It is far wiser to let children see the clay, the better to appreciate the few pieces of Parian marble and genuine gold that the idols may contain. The children would be less likely ever to become disillusioned, as did the generation of whose indifference to our national myths these critics complained. [39]

Of course, there is a more "positive" or "constructive" side to the reexamination of traditional accounts of events and views of individuals. Sometimes, by studying past data again and by accumulating later, previously unknown facts, we correct earlier conclusions that were unfair. For example, in *George Washington: The Virginia Period, 1732-1775,* Bernhard Knollenberg expresses the belief that there is a need "to refrain from undue glorification of Washington, not only to avoid a distorted picture of him, but because his glorification has often been at the expense of injustice to the reputation of others." [40] The largely distorted, negative, prejudiced view of Mary Todd Lincoln that so many lay people and scholars formed from the writings and speeches of William H. Herndon, Lincoln's law partner, have been moderated by more recent perspectives, such as one finds in *Lincoln Reconsidered* (1961) by David Donald [41] and *With Malice Toward None: The Life of Abraham Lincoln* (1977) by Stephen B. Oates. [42] But, setting aside people ranging from those who want to destroy every cherished belief to those who want to aggrandize everything that has happened, the reflective social studies teacher has little choice but to free and to help learners follow the evidence they gather to the conclusions it supports.

The teacher might set the stage for further investigation into historical misinformation, misconceptions, myths, and mysteries by reading aloud one of the entries in *The Dictionary of Misinformation* by Tom Burnam, such as this selection:

> "Barbara Frietchie." John Greenleaf Whittier's famous poem with its often quoted lines— " 'Shoot, if you must, this old gray head, But spare your country's flag,' she said" —which purports to tell of an actual episode involving Stonewall Jackson during the Civil War, must be taken with more than a grain of salt. According to an eyewitness, Jackson's troops never got within three hundred yards of Barbara Frietchie's home. Even if they did, Ms. Frietchie could not have "(taken) up the flag the man hauled down" and set it in her attic window. Whittier gives her age as "fourscore years and ten," but she was actually older: ninety-six. And she was bedridden and helpless, having lost the power of locomotion; she could move only with the help of attendants. [43]

Then, the teacher might read aloud to a high school class this portion of Thomas A. Bailey's preface to *Probing America's Past: A Critical Examination of Major Myths and Misconceptions:*

> ... My hope is that readers will develop an appreciation of how American history has been warped in the past so that they may be on their guard in the present. They should come away with a deepened awareness of the complexity of the historical process, the prevalence of pitfalls, and the folly of making easy generalizations. [44]

Immediately following the oral reading of the preceding, the teacher might invite two or three class members to volunteer to choose and to read aloud from among Professor Bailey's many topics, such as "Were the Carpetbaggers Northern Vultures," "Did Catholicism Defeat Al Smith in 1928", and "Who Started the Cold War?"

The secondary world history teacher might lead students into Josephine Tey's *The Daughter of Time* by telling the class this story:

> An English teacher informed a high school class that many successful novels contain some religion, some royalty, some sex, and some mystery. A student with a sense of humor asked his teacher if he had the general idea when he submitted the following on a piece of paper: "My God, the princess is pregnant! I wonder who done it."

Then, the teacher might hold up a copy of *The Daughter of Time* and say something like, "Here's a really good historical mystery novel that has it all. It tells about the treachery of Lord Stanley, the loose morals of Jane Shore, the magnanimity of Richard III, the duplicity of Lord Hastings, the consuming ambition of John Morton, and the shabbiness of Henry VII. In this book, a Scotland Yard inspector, recuperating in a hospital, and a young, amateur scholar try to find out whether King Richard III murdered his nephews.

"Would you like for me to read aloud from this suspense story a little bit each day; or should I ask the school librarian to get paperback copies of it for everyone so you can read it yourselves the next few weeks before we get into it?"

Following the reading of the book, the teacher might invite a discussion of this quotation before leading a thorough class investigation into whether the traditional story of the Richard III mystery is buttressed by the facts that have been uncovered and assembled over the centuries:

> ... It's an odd thing but when you tell someone the true facts of a mythical tale they are indignant not with the teller but with you. They don't *want* to have their ideas upset. It rouses some vague uneasiness in them, I think, and they resent it. So they reject it and refuse to think about it. ... [45]

Next, the teacher would stock a shelf in the classroom with all sorts of sources [46] relevant to the mystery. Assuming that there are thirty students in the world history class, the teacher might form five committees with six members each. Committee assignments could be determined by a drawing, using six squares of colored construction paper in five colors. Students with green squares would be agents in the Green Detective Agency, which might try to find out the answer to this question: "Where did William Shakespeare get the story for his popular play *The Tragedy of King Richard III*?" "Was Richard a monster with a crouchback and a withered arm?"

could be the question assigned to the Orange Detective Agency. The Yellow Detective Agency might look into "Did King Richard III order the murder of his nephews?" "Were the bones found accidentally in 1674, sealed in an urn, and then opened for examination in 1933 the remains of the young princes?" could be investigated by the Purple Detective Agency. And, the Brown Detective Agency might be asked, "Did Henry have the princes murdered?" After all the research has been conducted and organized, a Chief of Detectives could be elected by each agency and could report his or her group's findings to the total class while everyone takes careful notes. Finally, each student would take a piece of 8½"×11" lined writing paper, draw a line lengthwise down the middle of each page, write "FACT" on the left side and "FICTION" on the right, and set down at least five examples each of factual and fictional statements related to the mystery of Richard III.

This last historical detective approach is the final recommendation in this chapter and is somewhat similar to the preceding suggestion. This time, however, detective agencies would be formed around the interests of individual class members and might, therefore, range in size from one to six or seven agents and in number from five to thirty agencies. To get the class started, the teacher might list on the chalkboard a number of possible topics, framed as questions and involving historical misinformation, misconceptions, myths, and mysteries. The teacher could get some ideas from *40 Million Schoolbooks Can't Be Wrong: Myths in American History* [47] by L. Ethan Ellis. Ellis wrote his book for younger readers, and it could be used with many junior and senior high school students. Taking some of the myths identified by Ellis, the teacher might write them in the form of questions to be investigated, such as: "Were the Puritans puritanical?", "Was there a unanimous colonial uprising?", "Were the robber barons ruthless?", and "Did President Franklin Delano Roosevelt sell out the United States at the conference at Yalta?" As soon as class members get the idea, the teacher would record their suggestions for topics on the chalkboard. From this point on, I will make up some questions secondary students might like to probe, offer a few suggestions in respective notes regarding sources the teacher might secure from public and college and university libraries for various student committees, and end with an imaginary detective report read aloud to the class by the elected Chief of Detectives of one of the agencies.

In *The Gateway to History,* Allan Nevins observed, "Mankind dearly loves a good story, and dearly loves to believe it true." [48] The traditional Ann Rutledge story is surely one of America's favorites, for it is still repeated in Sunday newspaper supplements, popular magazines, and the like. Interested secondary students might form a class detective agency around the question "Was Ann Rutledge Abraham Lincoln's first and only real love?" A second committee suggests itself immediately: "Was Mary Todd Lincoln a horrible wife to Abraham Lincoln and a crazy person?" Obviously, it would be easy for members of the two committees to secure abundant material here, to trade information, and perhaps even to argue with each other for awhile at first. Since the two topics are so closely related, I have combined some of the best sources and listed them in alphabetical order at the end of the chapter. [49]

"Was President Warren G. Harding poisoned by Mrs. Harding?" is a possible detective agency question which clearly has the ring of a murder mystery to it. To start the agent(s) off on the wrong track, the teacher might recommend that *The Strange Death of President Harding* be read first. The committee member(s) can "solve" the case easily with the other books suggested. [50]

A number of interesting questions attend the life of George Washington, such as, "Was George Washington in love with Sally Fairfax?", "Did Martha Dandridge Custis Washington and George Washington have an unsuccessful marriage?", "Was George Washington a military genius?" and "Did George Washington serve his countries (England and America) without personal profit?" Books to match the last question may be found at the end of the chapter.[51] The teacher might launch an investigation here with this passage from the book *George Washington: Man and Monument* by Marcus Cunliffe:

> ...(Washington) detested shabby behavior in others, and could not bear that they should attribute petty instincts to him. Once before, as a gentleman volunteer under Braddock, he had shown his disinterestedness by serving without pay and without formal rank. He now repeated the gesture on a grander scale, by informing Congress that he required no salary; he would accept only his expenses...[52]

The Knollenberg book, though disturbing in places, should be read before *George Washington's Expense Account* by General George Washington and Marvin Kitman, Pfc. (Ret.), for the latter is rather shocking and irreverent, not to mention interesting and humorous.

"Was Herbert Hoover an unfeeling person and president who did not care whether millions of Americans were unemployed, homeless, cold, and hungry during the Great Depression?" might be still another question for a group of younger historical detectives to explore. In going through books suggested,[53] learners might encounter a number of revealing passages, such as this one, written by Arthur Krock, a long-time Washington correspondent and three-time Pulitzer prize-winner:

> A man came to dinner at my house in Washington one evening in the late 1950s, and his private personality was a stunning revelation to a company that had assumed the truth of most of the cruel criticisms that had been published about him. It was a sophisticated company, including diplomats, politicians in office and their wives. But nearly all had come to Washington after this particular guest's official tenure had ended.
>
> He was very relaxed that night, allowing full exposure to a high degree of social grace, anecdotal humor and wit, a keen analytical talent in assaying history, men, and measures, an unusual knowledge of remote places—yet all this with a dignity of bearing both innate and impressive.
>
> When he left, the wife of a Senator (who had furthered the false legend of a President who lacked the imagination and resolution to meet the acute problems of his time in office) exclaimed, "That just can't be Herbert Hoover!" But it was.[54]

As I indicated earlier, this last illustration of a question with which a student detective agency might deal is presented here as a fictional oral report:

> The question we—the members of my detective agency and I—liked and picked is "Did General Robert E. Lee surrender his sword to General Ulysses S. Grant at Appomattox Court House?"
>
> Well, first, the five of us just sort of read around—in textbooks and encyclopedias and short Civil War history books and stuff. You know what we found out? Just about everything! Like Lee gave his sword to Grant, and Grant broke it over his knee to show that that was the end of the war—and Lee offered his sword to Grant, but Grant, being a fellow officer and gentleman, told Lee to

keep it—and maybe Lee didn't have any sword—and for sure Lee had one of two different swords—and like that.

So, Tom and I went downtown to the big public library. The librarian in the part where they had the history and biography books was a nice guy. We told him our problem. He said, "You'd better get it from the horse's mouth!"— whatever that means. But he hauled out some books for us. One had letters by Lee, but we didn't find what we wanted. Another had some stuff put together by Lee's son, but we struck out again. We were beginning to take up too much of the librarian's time, we felt, so we said we had to go. He said to wait a minute longer. He got two more books, and we checked 'em out. [55] *When we got home, we found this in Grant's* Memoirs: *"The much talked of surrendering of Lee's sword and my handing it back, this and much more that has been said about it is the purest romance."* [56] *So, I said, "That's that." And Tom said we might just as well look in the other book as long as we had it. It was by Adam Badeau. He was some kind of general in the U. S. Army. And, he was Grant's secretary and aide. He said he was a personal witness to part of the story he was about to tell and that he would swear to the rest.*

Anyway, Badeau says that while Grant was writing the surrender letter for Lee to sign, Grant just happened to look up. He saw Lee's sword. So, Grant put into the letter that officers could keep their side-arms and horses and personal property. Lee had probably expected to give up his sword. But Grant spared Lee this "humiliation." [57]

That's all we found out. We don't have any answer for sure. But the Badeau version makes as much sense as other things we read. It seems to fit.

Conclusion

In *Historians' Fallacies: Toward a Logic of Historical Thought,* David Hackett Fischer writes, "Historians have a heavy responsibility not merely to teach people substantive historical truths but also to teach them how to think historically." [58] Borrowing on Fischer's phrasing, elementary and secondary social studies teachers have a heavy responsibility not merely to teach meaningful history and to teach learners how to think historically but also to teach children and youth how to *think*—period.

Notes

1. Robert L. Heilbroner, *The Future as History* (New York: Grove Press, 1961), p. 209.

2. Allan Nevins, *The Gateway to History* (Garden City, N. Y.: Doubleday & Co., 1962), p. 39.(Italics mine.)

3. C. V. Wedgwood, *Truth and Opinion: Historical Essays* (New York: The Macmillan Co., 1960), p. 15. (Italics mine.)

4. H. Stuart Hughes, *History As Art and As Science* (New York: Harper & Row, 1964), p. 6. (Italics mine.)

5. Ibid., p. 70. (Italics mine.)

6. John Higham, with Leonard Krieger and Felix Gilbert, *History* (Englewood Cliffs, N. J.: Prentice-Hall, 1965), p. ix. (Italics mine.)

7. Hughes, *History As Art and As Science,* p. 69.

8. Although American history teachers can use innumerable sources to inspire ideas involving chronological sequence and to check the dates of events, I relied here largely on a book that should be in every secondary school library and that a dedicated professional should own: Richard B. Morris, ed., and Jeffrey B. Morris, assoc. ed., *Encyclopedia of American History* (New York, Harper & Row, 1976).

9. Some of the best sources are Robert F. Cushman, *Cases in Constitutional Law,* 4th ed. (Englewood Cliffs, N. J.: Prentice-Hall, 1975); Robert F. Cushman, *Leading Constitutional Decisions,* 15th ed. (Englewood Cliffs, N. J.: Prentice-Hall, 1977); Stanley I. Kutler, ed., *The Supreme Court and the Constitution: Readings in American Constitutional History,* 2d ed. (New York: W. W. Norton & Co., 1977); William B. Lockhart, Yale Kamisar, and Jesse H. Choper, *Cases and Materials on Constitutional Rights and Liberties,* 4th ed. (St. Paul: West Publishing Co., 1975); Alpheus Thomas Mason and William M. Beaney, *American Constitutional Law: Introductory Essays and Selected Cases,* 6th ed. (Englewood Cliffs, N. J.: Prentice-Hall, 1978). Harold J. Spaeth has selected and introduced cases related to a theme in a series entitled *Classic and Current Decisions of the United States Supreme Court* (San Francisco: W. H. Freeman and Co., 1977), which would be very helpful for this activity. He deals with decisions related to obscenity in #28.

10. Quoted in Robert F. Cushman, *Leading Constitutional Decisions,* p. 411.

11. Ibid., p. 423.

12. Ibid., p. 425.

13. Mason and Beaney, *American Constitutional Law,* p. 496.

14. Alex Haley, *Roots* (New York: Dell Publishing Co., 1977). *Alex Haley Tells the Story of His Search for Roots* (Warner 2BS-3036).

15. For example, American Genealogical Research Institute Staff, *How to Trace Your Family Tree: A Complete and Easy to Understand Guide for the Beginner* (Garden City, N.Y.: Doubleday & Co., 1975); Charles C. Blockson and Ron Fry, *Black Genealogy* (Englewood Cliffs, N. J.: Prentice-Hall, 1977); Gilbert H. Doane, *Searching for Your Ancestors: The How and Why of Genealogy* (New York: Bantam Books, 1974); David Iredale, *Your Family Tree: A Handbook on Tracing Ancestors and Compiling One's Own Pedigree* (London: Shire Publications, 1972); L. G. Pine, *The Genealogist's Encyclopedia* (New York: Collier Books, 1977); Dan Rottenberg, *Finding Our Fathers* (New York: Random House, 1977); Harriet Stryker-Rodda, *How to Climb Your Family Tree: Genealogy for Beginners* (New York: J. B. Lippincott Co., 1977); F. Wilbur Hembold, *Tracing Your Ancestry* (Birmingham, Ala.: Oxmoor House, 1976).

16. The information used in my fictional oral report was secured from a pedigree chart reproduced in Neil Dougall, "Stallion Selection and Management," in *The Complete Book of the Horse,* ed. Elwin Hartley Edwards (New York: Arco Publishing Co., 1973), section 2, part 5, p. 161.

17. Joseph Nathan Kane, *Facts about the Presidents: A Compilation of Biographical and Historical Data* (New York: Ace Books, 1976), p. 358.

18. Eunice Kelley Randall, comp., *David O'Killia the Immigrant of Old Yarmouth, Massachusetts with His Descendants and Allied Families: 1652-1962* (Limited Edition Copy No. 187 of 500, 1962).

19. Centerville Old Home Week Association, *Old Home Week Celebration in Centerville, Massachusetts, August 19-22, 1904: Historical Notes* (Boston: The Sparrell Print, Limited Edition Copy No. 74 of 500, 1905).

20. Robin W. Winks, ed., *The Historian as Detective: Essays on Evidence* (New York: Harper & Row, 1969), p. xiii.

21. Ibid., p. 4.

22. John Dickson Carr, *The Life of Sir Arthur Conan Doyle* (New York: Vintage Books, 1975), p. 71.

23. Winks, *The Historian as Detective,* p. xxiv.

24. Fritz Stern, ed., *The Varieties of History* (Cleveland: The World Publishing Co., 1964), p. 29.

25. "Clue" is a detective game copyrighted (© 1949, 1950) by Parker Brothers, Inc., Salem, Massachusetts.

26. Donald J. Sobol, "The Case of the Two-Dollar Bill," in *Enyclopedia Brown Tracks Them Down* (New York: Pocket Books, 1977), pp. 58-64.

27. John D. MacDonald, "The Homesick Buick," in *Masterpieces of Mystery and Detection*, comp. Rosamund Morris (New York: Hart Publishing Co., 1965), pp. 135-55.

28. Ibid., p. 147.

29. Georges Simenon, "Mme. Maigret's Admirer," in *Ellery Queen's Crimes and Consequences,* ed. Ellery Queen (New York: Davis Publications, 1977), pp. 7-37.

30. Sir Arthur Conan Doyle, *The Complete Sherlock Holmes* (Garden City, N. Y.: Doubleday & Co., 1930), pp. 92-93.

31. At the intermediate grade level, the teacher might begin with a group of the Encyclopedia Brown books, one of which is cited in note 26. These books are still coming out, and younger readers pounce on the latest collections when they arrive at bookstores. A book which many fifth and sixth graders would like is *Key to the Treasure* by Peggy Parish, published by Collier Books in 1971. This is an excellent example of inductive "detective" work, and it relates especially well with history. In grades 5-7, *Uncle Robert's Secret,* written by Wylly Folk St. John and published in 1977 by Avon Books as a Camelot Book, could be used. Mystery books by Robert Arthur (including *Spies and More Spies, Ghosts and More Ghosts,* and *Mystery and More Mystery* and published by Windward Books) and by Phyllis A. Whitney (such as *Secret of the Missing Footprints, Secret of the Samurai Sword, The Mystery of the Gulls* and *Mystery of the Black Diamonds,* published by The New American Library under the Signet Book colophon) might be read by junior high school students. With developing historical detectives at the senior high school level, there are endless possibilities, of course. Each student in a class could read a different title by Agatha Christie, for example, including *Ten Little Indians* and *Murder on the Orient Express.* A number of years before her passing, Dame Agatha wrote two novels for posthumous publication. Hercule Poirot's last case is reported in *Curtain* (a 1976 Pocket Book), and Miss Jane Marple's concluding mystery, *Sleeping Murder* (Bantam Books, 1977) was Christie's 87th and final novel. *Cat of Many Tails; Double, Double; and The Fourth Side of the Triangle* are only three of a number of Ellery Queen books published by Ballantine Books. At least one of the Dashiell Hammett paperbacks published by Vintage Books, such as *The Maltese Falcon* and *The Thin Man,* should be included in the teacher's list of mysteries recommended to high school students. Harry Kemelman's Rabbi cases (*Friday the Rabbi Slept Late,* etc., Fawcett Crest Books) can interest and entertain better readers. *The Innocence of Father Brown, The Wisdom of Father Brown, The Secret of Father Brown,* etc. (Penguin Books) by G. K. Chesterton are especially well-written collections. John D. MacDonald is a creative and seasoned writer of thrillers, and Fawcett Gold Medal Books has published enough of his works to supply a class with different titles, including the Travis McGee series (*The Turquoise Lament, The Scarlet Ruse, Pale Gray for Guilt,* etc.). And, Dorothy L. Sayers is regarded as one of the top writers in the field. Her Avon paperbacks include *In the Teeth of the Evidence, The Documents in the Case* (with Robert Eustace), and *Murder Must Advertise.* Many readers like Sayers' Lord Peter Wimsey. In addition to *The Daughter of Time,* discussed later in this chapter, Josephine Tey books (*A Shilling for Candles, The Man in the Queue, Miss Pym Disposes,* etc.) have come out as Berkley Medallion paperbacks.

32. Figure 6-A is a footwarmer; hot coals were held in the little pan. Those are Conestoga wagon bells in 6-B. A bootjack (6-C) held the heel of a boot to help in the boot's removal. 6-D, of course, is a wringer to get some of the water out of clothes before hanging them out to dry. Clothes were stirred in hot, soapy water with this washing agitator (6-E). 6-F is a kraut cutter, used to shred cabbage. A candle dipper is pictured in 6-G. A photograph of pretty butter stamps appears in 6-H. Yes, 6-I is a flatiron. 6-J is a shoe (or jack) last which held a shoe in place while it was being made or repaired. No, one could not swat a fly very well with 6-K. It is a rug beater, designed to get out some of the dust. 6-L is a bedwarmer, not a cornpopper; and 6-M is a potato masher, not a pestle. A washing board is shown in 6-N. And 6-O is a gamel hook. (A hog was suspended upside down from the ceiling with the hind legs spread on the gamel hook's arms so the hog could be split down the middle by a butcher.)

33. A. A. Hoehling and Mary Hoehling, *The Last Voyage of the Lusitania* (New York: Dell Publishing Co., 1974).

34. Colin Simpson, *The Lusitania* (New York: Ballantine Books, 1976).

35. Ibid., p. unnumbered.

36. Ibid., p. 8.

37. Carl L. Becker, "What Is Evidence?," in Winks, *The Historian as Detective,* p. 6. Originally appeared in "Everyman His Own Historian," by Carl L. Becker, copyright © 1932 by The American Historical Association in *American Historical Review.*

38. Marc Bloch, *The Historian's Craft* (New York: Vintage Books, Alfred A. Knopf, 1964), pp. 136-37.

39. Louis Gottschalk, *Understanding History: A Primer of Historical Method,* 2d ed. (New York: Alfred A. Knopf, 1964), p. 7.

40. Bernhard Knollenberg, *George Washington: The Virginia Period, 1732-1775* (Durham, N. C.: Duke University Press, 1964), p. v.

41. David Donald, *Lincoln Reconsidered* (New York: Alfred A. Knopf, 1961).

42. Stephen B. Oates, *With Malice Toward None: The Life of Abraham Lincoln* (New York: Harper & Row, 1977).

43. Tom Burnam, *The Dictionary of Misinformation* (New York: Thomas Y. Crowell Co., 1975), p. 6. Entry on page 6 from *The Dictionary of Misinformation* by Tom Burnam (Thomas Y. Crowell).

44. Thomas A. Bailey, *Probing America's Past: A Critical Examination of Major Myths and Misconceptions,* vol. 2 (Lexington, Mass.: D. C. Heath and Co., 1973), p. vii.

45. Josephine Tey, *The Daughter of Time* (New York: Berkley Medallion Books, 1975), p. 136.

46. For example, Sir R. Markham Clements, *Richard III: His Life & Character: Reviewed in the Light of Recent Research* (New York: Russell & Russell, First Published in 1906, and Reissued in 1968); Thomas B. Costain, *The Last Plantagenets* (Garden City, N. Y.: Doubleday & Co., 1962); Paul Murray Kendall, *Richard the Third* (New York: W.W. Norton & Co., 1955, 1956); Philip Lindsay, *The Tragic King: Richard III* (New York: Robert M. McBride & Co., 1934).

47. L. Ethan Ellis, *40 Million Schoolbooks Can't Be Wrong: Myths in American History* (New York: Macmillan Publishing Co., 1975).

48. Nevins, *The Gateway to History,* p. 137.

49. Paul M. Angle, "The Case of the Man in Love: Forgery, Impure and Simple," (from "The Minor Collection: A Criticism") in Winks, *The Historian as Detective,* pp. 127-141; Bernie Babcock, *The Soul of Ann Rutledge: Abraham Lincoln's Romance* (New York: Grossett & Dunlap, 1919); Godfrey Rathbone Benson, Lord Charnwood, *Abraham Lincoln* (New York: Pocket Books, 1939); Donald, *Lincoln Reconsidered;* Emanuel Hertz, ed., *The Hidden Lincoln: From the Letters and Papers of William H. Herndon* (New York: Blue Ribbon Books, 1940); Oates, *With Malice Toward None;* J. G. Randall, *Lincoln the President: Springfield to Gettysburg,* vol. 2 (New York: Dodd, Mead & Co., 1946); James A. Rhodes and Dean Jauchius, *The Trial of Mary Todd Lincoln* (Indianapolis: Bobbs-Merrill Co., 1959); Carl Sandburg, *Abraham Lincoln: The Prairie Years and The War Years* (New York: Harcourt, Brace and Co., 1954); Philip Van Doren Stern, *The Life and Writings of Abraham Lincoln* (New York: The Modern Library, Random House, 1940); Irving Stone, *Love Is Eternal: A Novel about Mary Todd and Abraham Lincoln* (New York: The New American Library, 1969).

50. Bailey, *Probing America's Past;* Edwin P. Hoyt, *Spectacular Rogue: Gaston B. Means* (Indianapolis: Bobbs-Merrill Co., 1963); Gaston B. Means, *The Strange Death of President Harding* (New York: Guild Publishing Corp., 1930); Edgar Eugene Robinson and Paul Carroll Edwards, ed., *The Memoirs of Ray Lyman Wilbur: 1875-1949* (Stanford, Calif.: Stanford University Press, 1960); Francis Russell, *The Shadow of Blooming Grove: Warren G. Harding in His Times* (New York: McGraw-Hill, 1968).

51. Marcus Cunliffe, *George Washington: Man and Monument* (New York: The New American Library, 1958); Knollenberg, *George Washington;* General George Washington and Marvin Kitman, Pfc. (Ret.), *George Washington's Expense Account* (New York: Ballantine Books, 1976).

52. Cunliffe, *George Washington,* p. 72.

53. Anne Emery, *American Friend: Herbert Hoover* (Chicago: Rand-McNally & Co., 1967); David Hinshaw, *Herbert Hoover: American Quaker* (New York: Farrar, Straus and Co., 1950); Arthur Krock, *Memoirs: Sixty Years on the Firing Line* (New York: Funk & Wagnalls, 1968). Eugene Lyons, *Herbert Hoover: A Biography* (New York: Doubleday & Co., 1964); Dorothy Horton McGee, *Herbert Hoover: Engineer, Humanitarian, Statesman* (New York: Dodd, Mead and Co., 1959); Harris Gaylord Warren, *Herbert Hoover and the Great Depression* (New York: W. W. Norton & Co., Inc., 1967); Harold Wolfe, *Herbert Hoover: Public Servant and Leader of the Loyal Opposition* (New York: Exposition Press, 1956).

54. Krock, *Memoirs: Sixty Years on the Firing Line,* p. 122.

55. Adam Badeau, *Military History of Ulysses S. Grant, From April, 1861, to April, 1865, vol. 3* (New York: D. Appleton and Company, 1881); U.S. Grant, *Personal Memoirs of U.S. Grant, Volumes I and II: A Facsimile of the Original 1885 Edition* (New York: Bonanza Books, n.d.).

56. Ibid., p. 494.

57. Badeau, *Military History of Ulysses S. Grant,* vol. 3, p. 605.

58. David Hackett Fischer, *Historians' Fallacies: Toward a Logic of Historical Thought* (New York: Harper & Row, 1970), p. 316.

Index